Our Haunted Home in the Country:

A True Story

By Dale Scott

Copyright © 2018 Dale Scott

All rights reserved.

ISBN-13: 978-1-7974-8375-7

CONTENTS

Author's Note	i
Floor Plan	iii
Chapter One	1
Chapter Two	11
Chapter Three	15
Chapter Four	19
Chapter Five	25
Chapter Six	31
Chapter Seven	41
Chapter Eight	47
Chapter Nine	55
Chapter Ten	65
Chapter Eleven	71
Chapter Twelve	79
Chapter Thirteen	83
Chapter Fourteen	91
Epilogue	93

AUTHOR'S NOTE: This is a true story of events in a haunted home. My family lived in this house from 1976 to 1989 (13 years). I have presented this in a condensed format (about five years). Names and dates have been changed to protect the privacy of those who wish to remain anonymous.

-Dale Scott

FLOOR PLAN

North →

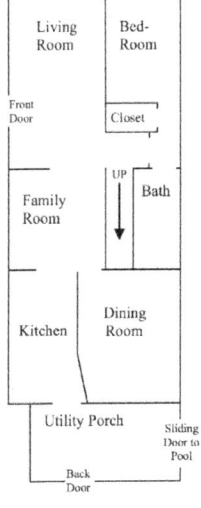

Downstairs

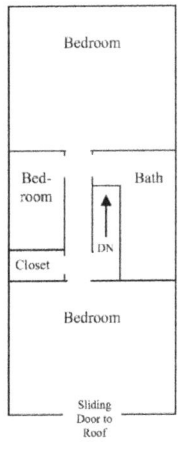

Upstairs

CHAPTER ONE

It was not an old house, or at least it did not appear to be. Unconventional construction techniques, while lending it charm, gave it an unfinished look. Some corners did not correctly meet. In some places, the outside of the house was made up of horizontal tongue-and-groove boards, while other parts had sheet siding. Not all of the windows had trim pieces around them. It looked like somebody's personal building project had been left undone.

Later, we were to find that this house was built upon a much older and smaller structure. The aging barns on the four-acre property should have been a clue that it was not as young as it appeared. What we saw was an early 1970's, A-frame two-story house with a dark brown cedar shake roof; exactly what we were looking for. I remember standing in the driveway the day we found it. The house looked lonely. The windows were like dark, sad eyes. It wanted someone to live in it. We saw many other places in our search--nicer, more modern houses--but this one beckoned us to live in it.

It was the end of spring in 1976, and I was fourteen. We lived in a small subdivision neighborhood in the western fringes of Santa Rosa, California, where all of the houses were the same, except for the paint color. It was a newly developed part of town and nearby pastures or small walnut orchards were giving way to neighborhoods like ours. Since the houses were close together, we knew most of our neighbors. Not all were friendly, but everyone knew each other by their first name. As for us kids, there were many children in the neighborhood, so we had many friends. Everyday, my sister Lisa and I would get on the school bus and wind our way through town to school.

This was the first house that Mom and Dad owned. They moved to Sonoma, California in the early 1960's from Oklahoma. Soon after, I was born, followed by Lisa three years later. I remember when our parents bought this house, but Lisa was too young to remember the little cottage we rented prior in El Verano, a "suburb" of Sonoma.

After buying the house in Santa Rosa, Mom and Dad started looking for another house. They wanted a place that required renovation, so that we could fix it up while living in it. They planned to sell it for a profit to supplement Mom's income from the music store, and Dad's income working for a local chain of grocery stores. I believe they wanted to continue buying and selling houses to make enough money to retire early.

We spent most of our evenings and Saturdays looking at houses. The majority of them were on the outskirts of town. One night, while looking through the real estate listing book, one entry intrigued us. It was a picture of a large house, and according to the description, it came with a considerable amount of land. Unlike the other places we saw, this house was quite far from the city limits of Santa Rosa. The most interesting thing, however, was the low price.

Mom and Dad grew up in rural areas. They knew what it was like to live in the country, but Lisa and I did not. The prospect of living away from town, in a place where the main activity seemed to be growing hay and raising cows, was inviting to us. One Saturday we all piled into our brown 1973 Ford Torino and went directly to the house to meet Jack, our real estate agent, so we could have a good look at the place.

The mid-day air was warm, and the wind from the open car window whipped my hair around. The short, barbed wire fences in this area were practically invisible in the tall grasses. It appeared as if there was one large mass of hay stretching between the oak-studded rolling hills. We saw farmhouses, fields and the old highway, but not much else. When the freeway was built during the early 1960's, this road became neglected and was only used by locals. There were no attractions, tourist or otherwise, to greet people travelling along this stretch of highway. The cars and trucks seemed to be of another age. We passed a couple of old gas stations that no longer pumped gas. One was converted into a corner store, and the other became a bar with neon beer signs in the windows. The peeling paint on the rusting metal buildings and gas pumps said a lot about how time had passed since that bygone era.

I expected to smell farm animal odors, but instead it was the light fragrance of the hay. The warm breeze was releasing the essence of the grasses, the same way hot water draws tea from leaves. During this time of year, the pale green color fades into the traditional straw yellow, and the swishing sound of the hay in the wind becomes more pronounced. After what seemed like a long drive, the car began to slow. Lisa and I popped our heads up to get a peek of the property as we arrived.

The view of the house and its surroundings from the highway resembled a lush green island in the middle of a sea of hay fields with only the very top of the roof poking through the greenery. It was stunning, and I felt excited to discover what was within. The house was bigger than it looked in the listing book, and the vastness of the fields around it was more than I could have imagined. All of the other places we viewed were small, and sat on tiny plots of land in unattractive surroundings. This place was beautiful.

I didn't get my hopes up right way, because I wondered if we could afford this kind of place. I asked Dad about it as we entered the gravel driveway. He said the asking price was very low for such a property, and that was why we were there to see it. It would not be easy for us to buy it, but Dad thought it just might be possible. He also said that it had sat empty for a while. It looked too good to be true--Dad's words, not mine. I held my breath, hoping that we could get it. As we continued down the driveway, the greenery began to close around us, and the golden grasses faded away.

The perspective was different in the center of the "island." We found the yards around the buildings overgrown with neglect. It was difficult to determine the intentions of the previous owners with respect to the landscaping. The front lawn was tall enough to reach the bottom of the windowsills. Except for two palm trees and two weeping willow trees, all of the plants looked like an entwined horticultural experiment. Jack wasn't there yet, so we decided to explore.

In the backyard, there was an ominous tree trunk that was once a large oak tree. What remained resembled a twelve-foot high wooden modern art statue of a person missing the head and arms. Behind it, a well-worn redwood fence encircled the backyard area. It had trace evidence of red staining that matched the barn next to it. In one corner was one of the palm trees, alongside a child's playhouse.

The front yard had a tall hedge of pampas grass, nearly the height of the house, which ran the length of its south side, along the driveway. Because of this hedge, and the trees next to it, the front yard was very private. Additionally, the blades (aptly named) of the pampas grass were razor sharp, preventing anyone from walking through the dense greenery to the driveway. As we explored, the lush vegetation surrounded us like a fortress, creating a near-silent isolation that was calming, yet unnerving at the same time.

While we were beginning to explore a shop that was built into the back of the barn closest to the house, Jack arrived. We didn't hear him coming up the driveway, so we were surprised when he pulled up to the open side of the old barn. He was a tall man who wore a large Texas-style cowboy hat and drove a big brown Lincoln Continental. His booming voice, reminded me of Robert Mitchum's. It had an honest sound to it.

"Howdy. I see you found the shop," he called out to us as he closed the door to his car. "Someone used to do carpentry work in that part of the barn. They even left some nails behind. But you gotta watch your head in there with that low ceiling. I don't know why they made it so low in there."

"Hi Jack," said Mom.

"So, Cathy, Burt, what do you think of the place so far?"

"It's big," said Dad, looking a little overwhelmed. "How far does the property go--all the way to the fences out there?"

"You betcha," said Jack. "You won't find a piece of land like this any cheaper either. This is a real steal at this price. Wait until you see inside the house."

On the way to the door, Jack pointed out the neglected Doughboy pool that was installed mostly in the ground, though it was designed to be built above ground only. He also pointed out the little water fountain pond made of concrete that was hidden in the tall grass of the backyard. I liked the deck surrounding the back of the house with its built-in benches. While Jack unlocked the door, he told us there was a full-sized fishing pond out in the field next to a giant poplar tree.

We viewed the utility porch first. In the corner was a little bathroom with a toilet and sink. The east and south sides had short but wide windows high on the walls, while on the north side of the room was a sliding glass door that opened to the deck around the pool. Even the back door had a large window in it. The position of the windows gave the feeling of being inside a lookout tower. While some people may consider this a fun adventurous feature of the room, my first thought was "what were they looking out for?"

The floor was mostly covered in white/gray linoleum tiles. Almost all were loose, and there were patches of dusty wood sub-floor where some of the tiles were missing.

"If it were me," Jack said, "I would just put Astroturf in here."

"I don't think so," was Mom's response, "maybe some indoor-outdoor carpet instead."

"That would do it. I bet that little bathroom is really handy when people are swimming," Jack said as he opened the wooden sliding pocket door to continue into the house.

We entered the kitchen, which was at least twice as large as the one we were used to. We passed through an eating area with large windows on our left, then into the center of the kitchen. The air was warm and felt thick in this room. All of the cabinets were custom made for the angular shapes of the room, and the tiled counter space was abundant. A window was above the sink, so one could look out over the front yard while washing dishes. One of the countertops extended into the next room as a little bar.

The family and living room areas were next. A bookshelf divider separated the large area into two rooms. There was an attempt to carpet this area, and the connected living room, but it looked like the installer ran out of carpet. The far west side of the living room was bare subflooring, with small pieces of plywood strewn about. There were no baseboards. It had an abandoned look, and it bothered me. The front door was on the south wall between two windows. It was difficult to open because of what appeared to be years of weathering. With a hefty push Jack got it open, and it was a relief to get some fresh air in the warm dusty rooms. Adjacent to the family room, was the dining room.

It was dark in the dining room, even with the curtains open. The air here seemed staler. Dark brown paneling as wainscoting surrounded the room, and the upper part of the wall was covered in semi-metallic gold wallpaper with red velvet Florentine designs. On the floor, textured red linoleum tiles made up a pattern that called out "conquistador-style." The one saving feature in the room was the large brass and crystal chandelier. The light shining through the many crystal pendants was mesmerizing. The only window in this room looked north over the swimming pool in the backyard.

After seeing the only downstairs bedroom (in the northwest corner of the house), along with its adjoining bathroom and walk-in closet, we continued to the second floor via an enclosed stairway. It was more like a hallway that went up. There were thirteen stairs. It wasn't until later that we counted them. Had we noticed at the time that the centermost feature of the house involved the "unlucky" number, I doubt it would have dampened our excitement. The stairs were covered with the same carpet found in the living room and creaked loudly when we walked on them. This stairway to the second story had no handrail, and a discoloration all along the wall at hand-level was evidence of the need for one. The top landing opened onto a hallway.

It was warm upstairs. There was a distinct smell of old wood, dust and stale air. We also noticed a rusty mineral smell, which we later discovered was due to the well water used in the house. It was obvious that the upstairs windows had not been opened for some time.

Three bedrooms occupied the second floor. Two of them had walls that made up the legs of an "A" because of the roof. They were at either ends of the hallway. The other was a small bedroom on the south side, across the hall from the oversized upstairs bathroom. The dormer windows in these rooms overlooked the front yard to the south, and the backyard and pool to the north. The east bedroom had a sliding glass door that opened to the flat roof over the utility porch, making a sort of deck. The edge of this flat roof was built around a small eucalyptus tree. A box had been cut out of the roof to let the trunk of the tree grow through it.

The only strange thing about the upstairs was the big bedroom at the west end of the hallway, with colors that frightened us. The carpet was a bright pink shag, resembling the colors of a strawberry cake with frosting and sprinkles. If this wasn't bad enough, the unknown decorator put wallpaper on the west wall that had vertical stripes alternating pink, orange, olive, and pale red. As a finishing touch, the lower sections of wall, before the ceiling made the shape of an "A," were painted with a high-gloss vibrant orange. Jack had plenty to say about this room. The words "rip up," "repaint" and "re-paper" were used frequently in his attempt to calm Mom and Dad. This spectacular sight marked the conclusion of the eleven-room tour.

As we walked back through the house to leave, in distant places within, we would hear "pops" and creaking. Jack attributed the sounds to the fact that the home had been empty for some time, and was settling from our walk. We all seemed satisfied with his answer and continued on our way out of the house.

Dad had some questions for Jack. Most were of a technical nature, but my ears perked up when he asked about the previous owners.

"Why are they asking so little for the house?" Dad questioned.

"Well, I'm not sure exactly. You can see the house is not in the best of shape. The family left in a hurry, and it has been vacant for almost a year," said Jack.

"What happened? Why did they leave like that?"

"I don't know exactly, but from what I've heard from the family's agent is that they were having difficulties with their kids. They were getting into some trouble, so they moved to another state."

"What kind of trouble?" asked Mom, curious to know more.

"Drugs, I think," said Jack.

With this, Mom quickly told Lisa and me to go explore outside for a while. We left while they talked in the kitchen.

My sister and I walked around the perimeter of the house, through the tall grass. We peered into the green liquid standing in the old backyard pool. The water was almost black, with foamy algae on the surface. A multitude of bugs, flying and swimming, had made this half-full pool their home. I felt an unexplainable uneasiness next to the pool, as if someone was watching us from the dining room. I didn't care. I thought that this was the "neatest" place we visited, and I hoped we would buy it.

When the adults were finished talking, we climbed into the car and waved goodbye to Jack.

"Don't wait too long if you want to make an offer. It looks like a real good deal to me," Jack advised Dad.

"We will call you in the morning to let you know," Dad replied.

"Thank you Jack," Mom added.

With this, Dad started the car and we drove out of the realm of the green "island," and back into the world we knew.

DALE SCOTT

CHAPTER TWO

All that night they talked. Mom and Dad were more excited about this house than any of the others. It sounded like they were working out some difficulties in order to make owning the house possible. This was a big decision for a couple in their early thirties with two kids. I also overheard them talking about how it seemed too good to be true, and that something must be wrong with the house. It didn't look good.

As I drifted off to sleep, I thought about how much fun it would be to live there. I dreamed about what it would be like to have all that space to play in--and a swimming pool. Images of exploring the barns filled my mind, and I drifted off, wishing we would get it.

When I woke up the next morning, I noticed a list on the kitchen table titled "Pros and Cons." As I began to read Mom walked into the kitchen.

"Do you like the house we saw yesterday?" she asked as Lisa walked in, half-awake.

"Oh yes," we both answered quickly.

"Guess what? We're going to try to buy it. If it works out, we're going to be moving!" Mom said enthusiastically.

She cautioned us about getting too excited since she

was not sure we would be able to buy it. Nevertheless, we were going to go ahead with it. She told us they were going to make an offer on the house the next day, Monday. We would know in a few days, or maybe a week, if it would be accepted. Mom explained that the whole process would probably take a long time, so we would just have to be patient. I didn't understand what the escrow process was at that age, but this is what she meant.

During the entire day Sunday, I heeded Mom's advice. I tried my best to look calm. The only way we could afford it was to make a low offer. Dad was sure they would not accept it because it was too low. We were all in a state of mild worry and suspense. Deep inside, however, I was thrilled and already thinking of which bedroom would be mine. Somehow, I knew that we would be moving.

It did not seem difficult to buy the house. Monday morning Dad asked Jack to make the offer, and by 5:30 that evening he called with the good news. Our low offer was accepted without conditions and no counter offer made by the sellers. We were amazed with the quick response. Dad explained he believed it was because the house sat empty for so long. All that was left was to prepare our old house to sell, and wait for escrow to close.

Mom and Dad were nervous about buying a new house without first selling the old one. Jack told them not to worry because the market was good. He was confident it would sell before we were ready to move and gave Dad a list of some suggested repairs to make it more appealing to buyers.

Jack urged my parents to tone down the bathroom. Mom and Dad created a modern art look in this room a couple of years prior. It had shiny orange paint on one side of the room and aluminum foil as wallpaper on the other with chrome fixtures and lights. Bead curtains matched the general orange color scheme. Next to the toilet Mom placed a sign she got from a friend in the restaurant business. It read "please wait to be seated." Being inside the room was like being in an orange Christmas ornament.

"Okay," said Jack with disbelief, "the only question I have is: why? This has got to go. Put this one on the top of your list."

So they stripped the foil, repainted the room, and removed the beads and the "please wait to be seated" sign. Dad fixed a soft spot in the floor by replacing some sub-floor and then recovering it with new linoleum. Afterward, it looked like any other bathroom.

We painted the entire interior of the house. The green shag carpets were professionally cleaned. Dad fixed the gate to the backyard, and we all helped trim and clean up to make it look nice outside.

Jack was preparing to put our house officially up for sale and enter it into the listings book. The night, before our listing was published, we received a phone call from a neighbor. She heard the rumor that we wanted to sell our house. Her brother wanted to buy a house nearby and was interested in ours. He visited us that night, toured our home, and made an offer. It seemed like someone or something wanted us in the new place. I wondered what was in store for us.

DALE SCOTT

CHAPTER THREE

Lisa, who was always strong willed, wanted the pink room, and she wanted the carpet and colors kept just as they were. I was surprised because she never really liked "cutesy" pink things. Mom and Dad looked at each other, puzzled, and gave their okay. Lisa was eleven at the time and she was so excited about her new pink room that she dashed upstairs immediately when we arrived on the first day. We could hear her walking around. I heard her talking upstairs, but didn't think much of it. A few minutes later Lisa came downstairs.

"Were you upstairs a few minutes ago?" she asked Mom.

"No, we've all been down here."

"I thought I heard someone walking around up there, and when I asked who it was, the walking stopped."

"Remember what Jack said? It's probably just the house settling. A big house like this makes noises sometimes," said Dad.

Dad inspected the carpet that was installed the day before we arrived. They carpeted the living room, family room, downstairs bedroom, and the utility porch, but not the stairs or any of the upstairs rooms. His friend Pat from work came over to help with the heavy moving. After surveying the rooms and deciding where things would go, we started unloading the boxes from the delivery truck that Mom borrowed from her store. There was plenty of room for our things.

The previous occupants left nothing, save a box filled with a complete set of encyclopedias in the dining room closet, and a plain envelope containing a letter written in a girl's handwriting in the downstairs walk-in closet. At first, it looked like the letter was left behind by accident, but on closer examination, it appeared that it was meant for us. As the piano and some of the heavier pieces of furniture were carried in, I sat up on the kitchen counter and read the letter:

"I don't want to leave here. I love this house. My parents are making us move to Idaho. We're moving because my best friend was killed in a car accident. I really miss her. It wasn't really an accident, but I don't want my friends to get in trouble. We're moving away because I won't tell."

I must have had some kind of reaction on my face, for my mother looked concerned and took the letter from me to read it for herself. She thought it was a sad letter, but we shouldn't let it bother us. We had more important and fun things to look forward to in our new house. I asked if we should tell the police about the accident in the letter, but Mom said not to worry about it. She quickly crumpled it and threw it away. Her face looked agitated, however, as she left the kitchen to help with the placement of the couch.

My parents decided to take the bedroom next to the upstairs landing. It was the one with the sliding glass door which opened to the roof above the utility porch; it had a walk-in closet. I was given the downstairs bedroom with a walk-in closet and bathroom adjoining. Everyone was content and excited at the same time. We reported our discoveries about our new bedrooms as we passed each other with boxes to and from the truck.

As it grew dark outside, the shadows became longer inside our new home. They seemed darker and colder than in other houses. The lights, except for the large fluorescent fixture in the kitchen, were dim and sparsely distributed. I felt uneasy in the dimly lit places when I was on my own. It felt like there was something in those dark recesses that did not want to be disturbed. No longer did I have the eagerness to explore these areas. This was a view of the house we had not seen, and I was worried that it was a mistake for us to move in.

Mom was determined to make our first evening a cheerful one. She sent Dad to pick up a big bucket of fried chicken, and we had a picnic on the floor in the living room. Although we were tired from moving boxes all day, the discussion during dinner reflected our excitement for our new home.

"Lisa, how do you like your new room?" asked Mom.

"It's neat! But I can't find my radio."

"I saw it over in that box by the front door," I said.

"How do you like your room, Dale?" Mom asked.

"It's big; I like it. But…"

"But, what?" Dad asked.

"Isn't it dark in all the rooms? It's okay in the daytime, but it gets creepy at night."

"Dale's afraid of the da-ark. Dale's afraid of the da-ark," Lisa teased.

"Don't worry. We're going to put in more lights and replace the dim bulbs with brighter ones. It will look much better," Dad's attempt at comforting me.

Somehow, I still had my doubts. Was it a superficial fear, or something that intuition was trying to tell me? I put it out of my mind, and we finished our dinner with a bit of peach ice cream (Dad's favorite). Afterward, we all went to our rooms to spend our first night in our new house.

There was a breeze that night. It didn't take much to rustle the trees and bushes around the house. Unfamiliar silhouettes of branches moving in the breeze became strange patterns on the walls. The house creaked often. It sounded like Mom and Dad were still working on things in the kitchen. I could hear the sound of utensils and dishes being put away. I did not fear the dark, but that night I found it difficult to sleep, and felt compelled to stay alert. As the night wore on, a fear began to build. Time continued to pass and I reassured myself that all would be all right. Should there be a problem, Mom and Dad were not far away. They were still unpacking in the kitchen when I finally drifted off around two o'clock.

The next morning I noticed that the kitchen looked the same as when we all went to bed. Mom was making breakfast, trying to find utensils and spices. Dad was outside with Lisa, looking at the yards. Everything appeared cheerful in the new day's sunlight. I mentioned during breakfast that I had trouble falling asleep. It turned out that I was the only one who couldn't sleep that night. Mom and Dad commented on how early and how quickly they fell asleep. Everyone slept through the creaking of the house and trees swaying in the breeze. No one was unpacking in the kitchen that night.

CHAPTER FOUR

Springtime was a special time this year. The warm weather was uplifting. Each day in our new place was an adventure, and I was part of it. The setting, with the barns, ponds and landscaping, transported me to another time-- an earlier time. We began our projects to clean and fix things up.

The tree in the front yard next to the driveway was like none I had ever seen before. It was a tamarisk tree in full bloom with a fuzzy pink blossom that was giving way to wispy fern-like greenery. Next to the tamarisk tree was an old climbing rose bush with white blooms. Its thorny branches and blooms were entwined with the branches of the pink tree, creating an arch-like opening between the lawn and the driveway. A large palm tree stood in the middle what was once a lawn. An acacia tree in the far corner of the front yard was finishing its yellow blooming cycle. Geraniums filled the brick planter all along the south side of the house, under the kitchen windows. They were tall and added bright reds, pinks and pure whites to the color scheme of the front yard.

The landscaping beyond the front yard, around the far side of the house, consisted of a small lawn that was surrounded with pine trees, oaks, eucalyptus, and bamboo. Fences and vegetation defined this secluded area. Beyond a small fence was the north side of the hayfield. A small gate connected this "side yard," as we called it, to the back yard where the pool was.

Each of the yards had distinctly different characteristics as did each room inside the house. While the "side yard" on the west side offered privacy, the back area with the pool was inviting in a festive sort of way. The front was more formal. And the fields that made up the rest of the property were vast and untamed.

In the center of the circular driveway, however, was a rose garden with a small redwood tree on one side and a weeping willow on the other. The rose garden also contained four enormous sand-colored boulders. Brilliant scarlet, yellow and white petals were exploding from the three rose bushes, leaving a thin blanket of hues on the ground that shimmered as the breeze passed over them. I took note of such things because, with the exception of setting up my own room, the yards were my sole project.

Mowing, weeding, trimming, raking and watering occupied most of my free time during weekends, but the result was worth it. When I started, I had to wade into the grass to find where not to mow in the different areas. I cut my arms attempting to trim the dead thorny branches that were bunching up on the trunk of the palm tree in the front yard. After a lot of work, it was becoming more park-like around the house and the yards began to reveal more of their intended grandeur. The colors and fragrances were invigorating. It gave me extra energy.

Along with the house, three buildings framed the circular driveway. One old barn was next to the utility porch. The wood that made up this structure looked almost prehistoric. Not only were the sizes of the boards bigger than modern lumber, but the edges were worn with age. The texture of the grain in these boards was well defined due to the affects of weather carving out the softer part of the wood. In the back part of the barn was the shop we noticed on our first visit. The ceiling in the shop area was low because a loft was built above it. This made it difficult to work inside the shop without banging your head. Someone in the past left an extensive collection of nails and screws, and we were able to use them for nearly any repair. Behind this barn was a large pile of scrap wood that was overgrown with weeds. Alongside the barn stood a large fenced-in dog kennel.

On the other side of the driveway was a longer barn that could hold four cars. We owned two cars, so Dad decided to use the back half for storage and the front half for the vehicles. There was a door in the back, and there was a small window in the middle of the north wall. The roof sagged somewhat, and the red paint was mostly faded from the outside walls, but it looked safe.

Behind the long garage was a building that contained two horse stalls and a chicken coop. The edges of the doors and feed troughs were worn from years of use with horses. There were strands of horsehair left behind in the rougher parts of the wood. Lisa suggested getting a horse, but for the immediate future, it would serve to hold up targets for B-B guns and arrows. This is something that we could never have done in the city. We were beginning to truly appreciate the space we now had to enjoy.

While the larger barns looked inviting from the outside, they gave off a different feeling inside. Each building had an oppressive coldness that persisted even on the hottest of days. I was afraid when entering them, as if something was waiting, hidden in the dark corners, watching me. Not wanting to take any chances, I made any required nighttime trips quick ones. At night, the long doorways, or any other openings, became thresholds between a dim light and pitch darkness. It was the kind of thick darkness that enveloped you like a gelatinous soupy substance.

The horse stalls, contrary to the other structures, did not have the dark feeling of the other buildings. There was an unknown attraction to play inside and around there. What was funny, however, was that the chicken coop was nailed shut. It was possible to see inside through a little window covered in wire fencing. I took a hammer to the stalls one day, and opened the chicken coop. The feeling inside was very peaceful. It was like a hiding place with a sort of tree-house feeling. Although puzzling now, at the time I didn't think of how strange it was that the small room had been nailed shut.

Out in the larger part of the field, north of the barns, was the pond. It was about sixty feet in diameter, and about fifteen feet deep. The poplar next to it was the tallest tree in the area. Previous owners made this a calm refuge. There was a place to sit and relax while watching Koi fish. As they swam in the pond, you could see the gold and silver bodies dart around below the surface. The leaves of the poplar would shimmer, and cattails in the pond would sway in the light spring breezes.

Lisa and I enjoyed playing here at our new house. The entire property proved to be a limitless hide and seek wonderland. Seemingly endless spring and summer days unlocked adventures for us. How lucky we were, and we knew it.

* * *

The following month was full of painting, minor repairs, cleaning, and tracing electrical circuits. In one crawlspace upstairs that stretched from a bathroom into the area behind of the pink room wall, there was an incredible tangled mass of wires. Most were actually in use, but quite a few went nowhere. In the kitchen were several electrical outlets, but only two of them worked. There were switches that didn't do anything. We felt a slight tingling when touching the edge of the kitchen counter. Through painful experience, we discovered it wasn't a good idea to touch this metallic edge under the ceramic tiled top, while holding onto any electrical appliance. Dad fixed the electrical problems, in some cases completely replacing wiring, and he was able to get all the outlets and switches in working order, with the exception of one outlet. Although we completed the electrical repairs, the lights continued to flash and flicker. We found fixing that was impossible.

The creaking and popping throughout the house also continued. Indistinguishable sounds would happen softly and quickly; just present enough for you to question if you had even heard them at all. Fragments of sentences, that were just beyond understanding, uttered from another room, disappeared like vapors whenever you followed them. Slowly, we were getting used to the quirks.

By June, the major projects were finished, and we began to settle into our new home. School was letting out for the summer vacation, and the family decided to take on a new project and revive the old pool. Dad overhauled the filtering system, added lots of water, and an array of chemicals. Lisa and I scrubbed the walls of the pool with a brush on a pole. It took several strong "shock-treatments" of chlorine, but after a week, the water turned clear and all the debris was vacuumed from the bottom. We even fished out a large oak branch. While we were scrubbing, Mom painted the surrounding red colored deck and its built-in benches brown. The pool appeared to have been neglected far too long. But now it was coming alive. The house was awakening, but we were slowly becoming asleep. We paid less heed to the odd noises and uneasy feelings. Dismissing them was getting easier and activities like fixing the pool helped to distract our attention. Things were, for the most part, pretty peaceful, and everyone was happy.

DALE SCOTT

CHAPTER FIVE

Then one day when I was home alone that first summer, I experienced my first shocking event. There was an old beat-up pick-up truck in our driveway, and the driver kept honking the horn. I did not hear it pull in. Normally we could not see anyone arriving down the driveway. If not for the honking, I wouldn't have noticed it there. I eventually got up the courage to go and see what the problem was. The driver was a frightening woman, cartoon-like in her mannerisms. She thrust a coffee-stained sheet of paper through the window at me. It was a form with the Census Bureau's letterhead on it, but she didn't appear very official to me. She demanded I tell her who lived in the house, threatening to take me to prison if I refused. I said nothing. I took the coffee-stained paper, ran inside and locked the door. At this, the woman angrily drove away in her truck, the tires kicking up gravel. Was that one of our neighbors? Why did she need to know who we were? If it was one of our neighbors, it was strange that we never saw her or the pick-up truck again.

Mom and Dad seemed quietly panicked when I told them. They tried to hide their worry while talking to me. Dad is a tall man, and not one to become unnerved easily.

Mom is very matter-of-fact when it comes to a crisis, but is generally cheerful and optimistic. So, I worried about their initial reaction. They made a new rule for Lisa and me to stay in the house if anyone drove up the driveway. This incident sparked a new awareness, and we began noticing other things happening around the house.

Things began to disappear. They would eventually show up, but somewhere else. For example, the bottle opener that went missing on Wednesday from the kitchen, would turn up on Saturday in the upstairs linen closet. The 5/8-inch wrench would be missing one day from the tool chest, and then appear in the silverware drawer with the spoons the following day. We didn't think much of this as we thought someone was playing jokes. A tension between family members began to rise because of this. The sentence "I don't have it" became far too common. The game progressed.

Soon bigger, more important things went missing: keys, books, jewelry. The music binders Mom needed for work started disappearing. When these types of things went missing, it was not funny. Mom and Dad had little patience when they could not find things they needed, especially when it looked like someone was playing a prank. They suspected Lisa and me. Once, some of Dad's razor-blade box cutters that he used for work were missing. The razors were deadly. I found them later, between bath towels in the upstairs linen closet, and one of them was open with the blade exposed.

At the time, none of us saw what was really happening. Our joyful enthusiasm for our new house was slowly turning to irritation and accusations of each other. Something wanted each of us to distrust--to become isolated. We were stronger as a family, than we were as individuals. What we didn't know was the "why." Why were we the targets? Why were these things going missing? Looking back, it was as if the house was a shy child that would not come out from behind her mother's skirt to say "hello," but would keep poking her head around while giggling. This "shy child," however, was only a disguise.

I suggested to my father that there could be another cause for all of the things to go missing. My theory was that something unseen was the cause for this activity. Although it made perfect sense to me, Dad would not hear of it. "We don't need to be making stuff up," he said, with sternness. The disappointment I felt because of this dismissal was overshadowed, however, by the concern that I was right. It frightened me more, knowing that I was alone in thinking there was another cause.

Of course, Lisa and I were home alone while our parents were at work. Since we were the only ones in the house during the day, I can see how they thought we were the ones hiding things. To avoid disciplinary measures, we would try to stall until we could find the missing articles. That didn't always work, and Dad forbade me to use the phrase "I don't know." As I was a slightly contrary kid at the time, I came up with another phrase: "I have no idea." There was no convincing them that something else was to blame. But then, there was the message.

We decided to go away on a picnic one Saturday. Mom purchased a new electric typewriter earlier in the week. It was a Smith-Corona cartridge system with an automatic platen return. We set it up next to the kitchen to test it out before leaving for the day. While Lisa and I played with the typewriter, Mom packed a large lunch of sandwiches, chips, iced tea and sodas. When she finished, we took the paper out of the new gadget and turned it off. We gathered some towels and put on our swimsuits. It was a beautiful warm summer day, and we were going to the Russian River.

About four o'clock we returned to find a torn fragment of an envelope in the typewriter. No one remembered leaving it in there. On the paper was a message:

Dear Scott family. . . .
I have taken something from you and…. you will never know what it was…
till it burns in HELL!

Mom, Lisa and I were sent outside to the car while my father searched inside for intruders. It took him awhile to search the whole place--a long while. We were holding our breath when he emerged from the back porch.

"It's alright. Nobody here. Come on in," he called from the back door. "There is no sign of anyone breaking in. All the windows are closed."

"What about someone with keys?" asked my mother in her matter of fact tone. I suspect she meant to give the appearance of calm by using this tone, but I always knew it meant serious concern, if not plain fear.

"We had all of the locks changed when we moved in, remember?"

They kept discussing it, but I knew who wrote the message. It was the house or something in it. It took things, and it would continue to take things. It had already taken more than we knew. The note said so.

We put the typewriter away. Although it was never discussed, from that point on, whenever it was used, we all instinctively put the typewriter back in its case as soon as we were finished. No more notes were left.

After the issue with the typewriter, we started to make lists of things missing: the last place we saw them, when they disappeared, when the objects were found and where. It was a bit silly. About two thirds of the listed items were explainable, but the rest were not. We never noticed anything that disappeared and didn't come back, except for a really nice soldering iron. This went missing from the tool cabinet a couple of years later, and even after everything was cleaned out when we moved away, it was never found. I don't think that there was any significant message intended for us in that particular item not showing up, but it was not found, and it was expensive. It did make me wonder, however.

We learned to accept this quirk, and learned to live with it. The more time that passed, the less we were alarmed. At that point, we would just let each other know what we were missing so that we could keep an eye out for it. We did not see the need to discuss it beyond that. I think we were afraid of the truth, and treating it more like a game and ignoring the cause, was a more comfortable way of dealing with it.

DALE SCOTT

CHAPTER SIX

As we settled into the house, and completed many of the immediate cleaning and repairs needed, we began to enjoy our new surroundings. Our larger plans for renovation were put on hold while we took time to relax during the early days of summer. There was no rush to start any remodeling projects. The house was ours, the weather was beautiful and we were happy.

In the warm summer days, the air was still, and heat radiated from everything. It was a kind of heat that made sounds seem to nearly disappear. Nowhere was this more apparent than in the fields. Wading into the tall grass meant swimming in this strange silence. The nearby sounds, such as footsteps in the grass, seemed louder than normal, and far off sounds were unnaturally distant. This near absence of sound could only be broken by a breeze.

On the fourth of July, we had our first big party in our new house. Many people came and the circular driveway was packed with cars. There were friends from both of the stores where Mom and Dad worked. In the little concrete fountain in the back yard, water sprayed upward, and then cascaded down a pile of stones before rejoining the rest of the water, only to be pumped back upward again. It was my project to get it going again, so I was proud to show it off that day. The main activities involved swimming in the revived pool, visiting with friends and a barbecue of massive proportions.

At one point, Mom played a practical joke on Dad, pouring out a large bottle of vodka into the planter, only to confess afterward that it was filled with water. Later in the party, the adults ganged up on Mom's boss and tossed him in the pool fully dressed. A roar of laughter started, and continued for a few minutes. During the laughter, a woman came out of the house and mentioned to my mother that the lights in the bathroom had burned-out.

It wasn't very urgent to replace the bulbs. After all, it was the middle of the day. Mom asked me to replace them right away just the same. I brought two bulbs from the kitchen cabinet and headed for the bathroom. When I reached the bathroom door, it was open, and both of the clear elongated hanging globe lights were on. They actually looked like four lights because of the mirror behind them. I turned the switch on and off, shook the globes, and I even beat on the wall near the switch with the lights on. They did not go out. They did not flicker.

I brought this to my mother's attention, and she asked the guest if she was mistaken. She seemed a bit offended, but confirmed she tried the switch several times. Mom then asked my father if he changed the bulbs. He hadn't, and the fact that I had taken the two bulbs out of a new full package, the only one we had left, confirmed this. Dad went outside to the back of the house, where the electrical panel was located, to check that the breaker had not been partially tripped. He said that they were all solidly in the "on" position. We thought it was strange, but did not think to consider it was connected to the "missing items" game. A week or so later, I began to wonder.

It was about 11:30 at night on a weekend, as I recall. I was watching a movie on the little black and white television in my room. Beyond the TV screen, I noticed the lights were on in the bathroom. They were off a moment before. I looked up to see who came downstairs to use the bathroom. No one was there. I hadn't noticed the light switch making its normal loud "click" sound. My heart began racing when I remembered the woman from the party having trouble with the lights. I called out and asked who was there. There was no response. I jumped up, but found that the door separating the bathroom and bedroom from the rest of the house was still closed.

I quickly opened the door to check the rest of the house. Looking around, I found myself to be alone. I went upstairs and checked with Mom and Dad. They had not been downstairs, and they had not seen Lisa go downstairs. A bit shaken, I turned on all the lights downstairs to be certain there was no one else. I didn't find anyone. Had I left the light on? I left my bedroom door open for a change, turned the light off and tried to sleep.

The next morning I was surprised to find that I slept well. My room in the light of day was cheerful, unlike the heavy feeling in the dark stillness of night. I got up and worked my way toward the kitchen. Dad was still finishing his coffee. He looked up from his paper.

"Good morning."

"Good morning," I said.

"I turned off your bathroom light this morning when I got up. You've got to remember to turn it off when you go to bed."

"I did turn it off. Maybe someone else turned it on."

"Your sister and mother are still asleep."

"I did turn it off," I said, puzzled.

"Well, it didn't come on by itself."

"I don't know how it came on."

"All I'm saying is to turn it off next time. It wastes electricity, and it costs money."

I said that I would check the bathroom next time, and we didn't mention light problems for a while. They did not go away though.

There were other things electrically that were strange, but could not really be classified as out of the ordinary. For example, both of the lights in that same bathroom burned out simultaneously. This time the bulbs actually expired. Once, while descending the stairs, the light bulb burned out while I was halfway down, as I was just passing the light fixture. The flash next to my face startled me. Lights would flicker in the chandelier in the dining room often. Most lights flickered at one time or the other. Once we came home at night to find all of the inside lights on downstairs, when no one could remember having left them on. We would either explain such things as faulty wiring, faulty bulbs, or simply as forgetfulness.

Because of the many possible rational causes of the incidents, we did not spend much effort trying to explain what was happening. I thought it was probably nothing and that it would just go away--or at least not get any worse. That was my hope.

* * *

The summer days in the country were far different than those I'd known growing up in the little city of Santa Rosa. The warm breeze across the dry hay fields blended with all of the flowers and greenery around the house, filling the air with a magical scent. The days were slow, and long. I would spend my time swimming, helping in the vegetable garden, mowing the lawns, and wandering by the pond. There was a grass fire on the nearby hill that summer, and we watched the aerial firefighters extinguish it by dumping orange borate on the flames with their World War II era bombers. Also, slight changes in the weather would dramatically change the mood of the environment. For example, after a brief rain shower, scents became different, lighting took on a different cast, and the colors changed allowing previously muted tones to shine. It was like being on vacation whenever you were home.

In late August, we were preparing to start school again. An unusual heavy rain with thunder and lightning passed over one warm afternoon. I had developed a new appreciation for jazz music over the last few months. That day I found a radio station playing some old jazz standards from the fifties and sixties. I popped a cassette in to capture the moment, and on the tape it is possible to hear the lightning strikes as they cause static on the radio signal. It was the last memorable event of the summer for me, and I often listen to that recording to remind me of the peacefulness. August was ending and it was time for school to start.

On the first day of school, I did not want to leave the security of our home for the unknown halls of Healdsburg High School. I did, however, meet one of our neighbors on the bus that day. She spoke crudely, and didn't look very clean. She was older and although I was used to the smell of Mom and Dad's cigarettes, her clothes reeked of smoke.

"You live in that house?"

"Yeah," I replied.

"I'm Samantha."

"Hi, I'm Dale."

"I knew the people that lived there. They were weird."

"They were? What do you mean weird?"

"I don't know. Just weird, you know? They moved away to some other state."

Samantha and I never became friends. In my opinion, she was the weird one. Therefore, I figured that the previous people in our house must have been okay. The bus eventually found its way to the school. I never really talked to Samantha after that. I didn't want to. I wished that she shared the same disinterest, but no.

I walked into a different world when I reported to the gymnasium for the first meeting of the school year. Later I found that I mistakenly sat in the seniors' section. Have you ever noticed how no one tells you these things? "Oh, by the way, you should sit with the other freshmen kids in the far corner underneath the painting of the greyhound." Instead, I picked the worst place in the entire gym - under the ten-foot painted "H."

The air was full of cigarette smell and alcohol. The guys in this section were hollering and cussing. They were spitting chewing tobacco under the bleachers and onto the wooden gym floor. Some guy slapped me on the back and offered me some Jack Daniels. When I politely declined him, he was quick to call me a rather crude synonym of "coward." Coming from a small private school in the city, this scene was eye opening.

Though I later met other people and grew to like the school, I always looked forward to going home at the end of the day. There were gangs (city officials denied the existence of them) roaming the halls in packs. Zoot-suited gang members called out threatening things to passing students, and unlike most people, I joked around with them. Somehow, I found a way to do that while remaining respectful. I think it was for this reason that they had a mutual respect for me, even when others didn't. Becoming acquainted with one of the leaders of these gangs proved to be the smartest move I made in those early days at Healdsburg High School. It was a relief to be able to tell a threatening gang member that "Jimmy" (the "godfather" of the gangs in that area) was a friend of mine. Still, when I arrived home each day, it was a tremendous relief. It was a welcoming haven despite the strange happenings in the house.

During the fall, the lights continued to flicker and things would continue to disappear and reappear. By this time, we were used to the house and its quirks. At that time, it was still not frightening.

I guess it was like the "frog in hot water" parable. If the water is heated gradually, the frog doesn't notice the heat and cooks, instead of jumping out of already heated water. We never noticed enough to want to jump out of the water. Looking back, we should have questioned the significance of the activities and left the place. None of the abnormalities really crossed the threshold into serious danger, so we thought it illogical to move, based on what we were experiencing.

Just before Christmas, Lisa and I returned from school to find that the sliding glass door by the pool was open. We went inside and saw that everything was a mess. The Christmas presents were opened and some were missing. Also missing were several things like the TV and some musical instruments. The closets were emptied and the clothes left on the floor. Drawers were opened and things were hanging out of them. Some windows were open, with the curtains blowing around. Our home had been burglarized. I picked up the phone, dialed "0" for the operator, and asked for the sheriff.

The rest of the evening was spent with a team of people taking photographs, looking for fingerprints, and taking lists of missing items. "I only touched the phone," I repeatedly responded during the evening. There was a lot of coffee made that night. When they left, we had a short family meeting and discussed our feelings about what happened.

Although this was most definitely the work of a real person, it nearly destroyed the sense of security we had. From this point forward, we were suspect of any unexpected activity around the house. Any strange car, unknown persons or even irregularities in the mail made us uneasy. Dad advised Lisa and me to call the Sheriff whenever anything was out of the ordinary. We posted the number for the Sheriff's Dispatch office next to the phone (there was no 9-1-1 at that time). Mom and Dad didn't want to take any chances when it came to our safety.

This burglary set a tone for our first winter, and that was magnified by the house's own mood. While everything was bright and cheery in the spring and summer, it became equally gloomy during winter months. The angle of the sun dropped further into the surrounding landscape, and the rooms were full of shadows. Once Christmas and New Year's Day passed, we set sail across a dark sea on our way to a far off land called spring. The days seemed heavy and slow, and we had no choice but to endure them.

Football season was finishing, and Lisa and I started the second half of the school year. Lisa had a birthday (mine was in October). In the later part of January, Mom gathered us together to tell us the great news that she was pregnant. She and Dad were very happy, and Lisa and I looked forward to a new brother or sister. Mom started preparing the small bedroom upstairs as a nursery.

This was the room across from the upstairs bathroom. There were two chests of drawers built into the wall. The strange thing was how they were fitted into the wall. The drawers went right into a crawlspace inside the wall. If you pulled the drawers out, you could see the dark void between the interior wall and the roof. I think this is the main reason that I found the room foreboding and creepy. But when Mom redecorated in anticipation of our new sibling, it took on a safe serene feel that dispelled the gloominess which troubled me.

During the winter, I noticed that the rooms had a stale smell to them. It wasn't a moisture odor, but a very dry dusty one. We would frequently open doors and windows to air out the house, but the smell persisted. This odor would move about the house. Sometimes a "clean" smelling room would go stale while we were in it. At night, the air in these stale spots seemed to have a soupy thickness. That part of the room would seem darker. I didn't like having to wade into these spots at night. The stale air added to the dreariness of the house during these seemingly long months.

The irregularities with the lights became more pronounced. Usually if you left a light on in a room and went elsewhere, when you returned it was dark in that room. Although it was rarer, lights would be on in a room you remember being dark moments before. Since it happened when no one was looking, I thought it was my imagination.

As the months progressed, spring began to creep back in. There were no plans made regarding the renovation and sale of the house. I thought we would start some kind of repair project that spring, but somehow that goal was fading. I asked Mom about it, but she changed the subject.

We became content. We loved the house, and that meant that the need to use it as a commodity to create wealth was dropping by the wayside. Spring was coming, the house was magical, and we were under its spell. With the blossoming flowers and new plant growth, the house and surrounding area awakened from gloominess.

DALE SCOTT

CHAPTER SEVEN

Similar to the previous spring, an unknown car appeared in the driveway. I was in my room in the back of the house therefore, I did not hear the car pull under the pink blossom tree. It was a Saturday, and Mom and Dad were both at work. Lisa was upstairs in her room playing. I was trying to figure out what to do when I remembered that Dad told us to call the Sheriff whenever anything strange happened. I carefully called up to Lisa. Luckily she heard me, came downstairs, and waited sitting on the stairs out of sight of the windows.

I looked out through the edge of the curtain and saw an older large maroon sedan. It was as big as a long Cadillac, but it looked more like a 1970's Buick or a Pontiac Bonneville. The paint was oxidized, making the overall color to appear bruise-like. All of its windows were down, and the car was empty. I didn't see anyone walking around. This frightened me, so I called the Sheriff. As the dispatcher finished with me and I began to hang up the phone, I saw a figure pass by one of the back windows in the living room. The figure was headed for the side yard in the back. I ducked into my room, got my baseball bat, returned to the stairs, and waited with Lisa for the sheriff.

Sweat was getting into my eyes and I could barely hear with the sound of my pulse in my ears. I was trying not to look scared. I didn't want to frighten Lisa. Tightly gripping the bat, I started to plan my defense. Surprise was my only hope for success. The sweat was now dripping from my hand down one side of the bat. We heard a noise coming from my bedroom. I took a deep breath, and prepared the bat. I told Lisa to go hide in her bedroom wardrobe. Then, for a couple of minutes there was silence. My blood was throbbing in my head, and my clothes were soaked in sweat. I kept listening carefully for any clue of where the figure might be. I heard a little sound outside by the front yard, then a loud knock on the door. I prayed. I asked for victory over the figure. I took another deep breath. The knocking started again, but louder. This time it was followed with a voice.

"It's the Sheriff's Department. Anyone home?"

I went to the window and looked out through the curtain. The long bruise-colored car had been replaced with a Sheriff cruiser with all the lights flashing. I carefully opened the door. I was so relieved to see the tall deputy in his khaki uniform, that I almost collapsed in the entryway.

"You can put the bat away now. Are you okay?"

"Yes, but pretty scared," I said shaking.

"I don't see any car. Where was it?"

"It was right where your car is parked now. I didn't hear it leave."

"Well I've been here for a couple minutes, and I didn't see anyone leaving when I pulled in your driveway. What did the car look like?"

"It was a big old long car. It was purple and a little beat up."

"How old would you say it was? Like a classic car or something?" he asked.

"No. It was like an early 70's car or maybe late 60's."

"Well, it might have been someone lost or something."

"I don't think so," I replied, "because whoever it was

went around back. I saw someone go past the windows."

"Okay. I'll walk around and check. Are you sure nobody got inside?"

"I didn't see or hear any one get in the other door in the back."

"Okay. I'll check the back door to make sure while I'm at it."

"Sorry to have to call you. There really was someone here."

"Don't worry. You call whenever you need help. That's why we're here."

The deputy walked around outside and checked all the bushes and any hiding places. He came back around to the front door to say that everything looked okay, and to call again if the car came back. With that, he walked to his car, turned off the flashing lights, wrote some things on his clipboard, closed the door and drove away.

I locked the front door, and checked the back door lock again. I called Mom to tell her what happened and what the deputy said. She thought everything would be all right until she got home, but if anything strange happened, we were to call the Sheriff again. It looked like things were okay at that point, so she was not worried.

It would be three hours before Mom was due to come home from work, and longer for Dad. This time passed slowly. I was consumed with nervousness. I went from the front windows to the back watching for the figure to return. Lisa and I kept the sound on the TV low to be able to keep an ear open for any sign of cars pulling up the driveway. Oddly, Lisa didn't appear to be that scared, or at least not as scared as I was. I jumped when we heard the sound of a car arriving quickly in the gravel driveway. I went to the kitchen window with the baseball bat. It was Mom.

That night after dinner, when everything calmed down, I could hear Mom and Dad in the dining room discussing what to do about the situation. Mom considered quitting her job to stay home to watch us. Dad didn't think that was necessary, but he suggested we stay with friends after school. Somewhere in this discussion, Dad had the idea to get a guard dog. That seemed to be something mutually agreeable.

The next day when Dad came home from work, he brought Hans, a large German shepherd that he found in the "want-ads" of the local newspaper. His owners were moving away and could not take him. He was well trained and gentle with us kids, but he absolutely didn't like men in suits. Dad built a nice large doghouse in the kennel area next to the old barn for Hans. With a long chain, he could wander around the entire side of the barn and into the driveway when we were not at home, and he would be safe from wandering off and being hit by cars on the road. Mom and Dad felt better knowing that Hans was there to protect us.

Every day when we got home from school, I would walk Hans outside and practice his training routine. "Heel. Sit. Down. Stay. Come." One day, while we were walking by the pool, he looked up at the dining room window and froze. He started barking aggressively. I didn't see anyone in the window. On later occasions, he barked at other things we couldn't see. We didn't think much of it. We just called him a "silly dog" for barking at nothing. He wasn't being "silly" though. He saw something we could not. This ability proved to be problematic.

It was the beginning of May. Mom and Dad were coming home late from an event at Mom's store. Dusk was quickly fading into a moonless sky when Hans started barking. He kept on barking. I switched off the TV and Lisa turned off the lights. Together we quietly went to each window, carefully peering out to find why Hans was barking. In the last remaining light, we thought we would at least see something moving. We did not. Next, we turned the outside lights on, but still there was nothing obvious. Hans stopped barking.

After this happened on a couple of other occasions, we knew we could not rely on Hans to alert us of an intruder. If he barked at things you could see, as well as things you could not, we would never really know if we needed to call the sheriff. We almost grew to ignore his barking. It did, after all, scare away almost anyone that began walking down the driveway from the highway. So he would bark, we would pause and then go back to whatever we were doing.

On one particular night in the last part of May, Hans again started barking. We were all in the family room watching television. We turned the TV off for a moment, but didn't hear anything outside. So we turned it on again and continued watching. A few moments passed when we heard a thud against the back wall of the house. The TV went off again and Dad told us to go hide. Mom went with us to Lisa's room upstairs, and Dad stayed downstairs. I could faintly hear him calling the sheriff as we approached the bedroom. In Lisa's room we didn't speak. I tried to listen carefully, but the blood rushing through my ears made the silence sound like quiet, dull television static. That noise was soon broken by the sound of sirens. Two sheriff cars had arrived.

I could hear Dad telling them what happened. Mom said we could all go back downstairs, so we went down and sat in the living room with Dad. While we waited, we saw flashlights going around the house. Dad said they brought the K-9 unit to help them search for the intruder. Through the window, I could see the patrol car spotlights scanning the fields around the house, and the deputy with the dog searching all around the outbuildings. There was a knock on the door. The deputies found no one. They did, however, find a place where the tall grass had been disturbed. The deputies thought whoever was lurking around the house managed to leave by that way, and somehow avoided being seen when their patrol cars arrived. Dad thanked them and they left. We locked the door and went back to watching television. No one said much. We were all thinking the same thing: how could they have missed someone hiding out there? They would be completely exposed in that field. Certainly the dog would have found anyone hiding. We tried to get lost in the TV show to take our minds off it.

The next day we found the place the deputies mentioned. It looked like a trail that went underneath an abandoned fence project in the side yard. It used the tall pine trees as posts and fence rails were in place, but no planks. The tree branches and some loose barbed wired covered most of where planks would be needed. Dad took an old 2x4 and nailed it to the place where the trail was created so that it touched the ground. The strange thing was that nothing else around that spot was disturbed. The tall grass around the fence was not flattened. If someone had used that as a trail, how did they do it without leaving any other trace?

We all were very nervous at this point. Because of the possibility of intruders, we would jump at any odd noise and check it out. There would be a pop here or there in the house, and little noises outside would catch our attention. Outside lights were added so that the entire perimeter of the house could be lit, when necessary. We became very aware of our area. No longer were we complacent and oblivious. We started listening carefully. Unfortunately, we began to find sounds that could not be explained.

CHAPTER EIGHT

During the summers, when it was warm, my sister and I became afraid to stay at home alone. It wasn't as much the threat of an intruder, but we felt uncomfortable in the house. Anything other than silence made us jump. It was a struggle to ignore things. Our normal everyday activities gave way to feelings of fear and worry. We just accepted it.

These fears were, of course, augmented at night. We would hear sounds in the living room while doing the dishes, therefore we began leaving the lights on. Then we would hear sounds in the downstairs bathroom. We turned those lights on as well. Soon, most of the lights downstairs were regularly lit. On several occasions, Dad was upset with us for lighting up the house "like a Christmas tree." Finally, Dad acquiesced and allowed us to turn on the little spotlights in the living room, but only very dim to save electricity.

I was ashamed of being afraid of the dark, so I always tried to play it down. We all played things down. Perhaps we thought that the problems would go away if we ignored them, or at least tried to ignore them. That may be one of the main reasons we tried to endure it. At any rate, leaving the house did not seem like a necessity, especially without concrete reasons. I could hear the explanation: "The roof wasn't falling in, and yes it was a dream house, but we heard sounds and we left." It didn't make sense. So we took note of the sounds and odd feelings, but continued living there in spite of them.

In late July, I was home alone. I don't remember why I was alone. I was cleaning my room (an odd occurrence in itself according to my mom). I needed something from the utility porch, so I crossed through the living room to get there. As I did so, I heard what sounded like a drawer being closed in Mom and Dad's room. I stopped and listened. I heard it again. I debated calling the sheriff. I knew how many times they had been to our house and was afraid that this would also turn out to be nothing. I summoned up my courage and decided to check it out. It was, after all, probably nothing. Then I debated the possibility that I was wrong and that there was somebody upstairs that was potentially dangerous. After some serious consideration, I grabbed my baseball bat from the closet and took a deep breath. I walked carefully up the stairs. I was about two thirds up when a step creaked loudly. The drawer sound stopped abruptly. I charged up the remaining four stairs and went in Mom and Dad's room. No one was there. The drawers were all in order, with no items hanging out of them. I looked into the walk-in closet. I checked the small bedroom. I checked the bathroom. Finally, I checked Lisa's room. No one. There was no way for anyone to get past me. I saw nobody, and there was no place else to hide. I was relieved not to find anyone. I was terrified that I didn't. I gave up and went back downstairs.

I kept the bat with me, just in case I was wrong, but I didn't see how anyone else could be in the house. I began to doubt my sanity. Had I really heard the drawers, or were my ears tricking me? About 15 minutes had passed when I heard the drawers again. This time they were louder, with more hurried activity. There was no doubt about it. These sounds were real, and I was going to find out "just who the hell it was."

I sprinted back up with the bat, ready for a fight. Again, there was nobody upstairs, and no trace of disturbance with the drawers. Although there was no way for anyone to leave through any of the windows and not be seen, I went out to the upper deck and checked the roof. No one.. I considered checking the attic, but the access door was in the ceiling of Mom and Dad's walk-in closet at the top of the stairs. It would be impossible for a person to get up there without being seen in the time that it took me to get up the thirteen steps. Then I checked behind the clothes in the closet. Carefully using the bat, I pushed the clothes aside, but it revealed no intruder.

I went back downstairs again, and as soon as I hit the bottom landing, the drawers started again. "STOP IT!" I screamed using all of the air in my lungs. The sound stopped. I took a replenishing breath and heard the air enter my body, but that was all I heard. There was near silence. The noises upstairs were gone. Shaking, I walked away from the stairs. Then, the sounds resumed with the drawers opening and violently slamming shut this time. I ran out of the house.

I could hear the slamming from the driveway. I looked up toward the roof and through the sliding glass door in their room to try to see what was happening. I saw nothing. No person. No moving drawers. Nothing. Then the sounds stopped. I waited.

I didn't like this game. I was tired of going up there and finding nothing. Once again, I mustered up my courage, went inside, but this time I put the bat back in my closet and stayed downstairs. Whatever was up in that bedroom, in my opinion, could go on making noise, but I wasn't going to check again. I turned the radio on in the kitchen, the volume loud so I wouldn't have to hear the sounds upstairs. It stayed quiet upstairs for the rest of the afternoon.

As far as I can remember, this was the first overt action in the house that could not be explained by logic. When Dad came home, I told him about it. He didn't believe me. The fact that I tried to confront a possible intruder upset him. He said the sounds were from the house settling, and it was natural. This was usually his response. He didn't believe in the supernatural. He didn't believe in ghosts. Although it was hard to hear it then, now I am thankful that Dad was a skeptic. For when the events happened to him and he said it was real, it meant something.

Before continuing with Dad's first major encounter, the following description is necessary. We had a "deep freeze" chest freezer in the utility porch. It was a great freezer, but it had the most hideous screech when you opened it. We tried greasing the hinges, but it didn't remove the "fingernails on the chalkboard" sound it created. Also, there was a mild quirk with how the upstairs hallway was built. The landing, as well as Mom and Dad's room, had a higher floor than the rooms to the west of the stairs. A six-inch ramp was constructed to compensate for this difference in the floor levels of the hallway. In addition to this unevenness, the hallway floorboards under the carpet were a little loose. Even the lightest of footsteps could be heard downstairs loudly. In effect, it was impossible for anyone to sneak across the upstairs hallway.

Dad was home alone this time. He was reading in the family room. From what he said, there was someone walking from my sister's room to his bedroom. When the footsteps reached the end of the hallway, they stopped. He heard the door to his bedroom open with a squeak. He put down his book and ran upstairs to find out if anyone was there. And, as was the case with my experience, he found nothing except the open door. He went downstairs and picked up his book again. As he started reading, he heard the footsteps returning to Lisa's room, and her bedroom door closing. He went back up. He found nothing, except that the door to Lisa's room had indeed been closed since his last trip. He rechecked every room, and as he was starting downstairs, he heard the screech from the door opening on the deep freeze in the utility porch, and the subsequent closing of the door with a bang. He ran to the porch. There was nothing out of the ordinary. The back door was still locked. After checking inside the freezer to see if someone was hiding inside it, he ran outside to see if anyone had fled on foot. There was no one.

After this, he began questioning a lot of what was happening in the house. The events could be denied no longer. When the rest of us came home, we had a family meeting. In this meeting, we agreed there were many things about our house we couldn't explain. We decided the house was haunted by something. Dad was to perform research on the house to learn its history. Mom suggested that we find out if there was a ghost and try to talk to it. Her theory was to share the house. To close the meeting, Dad told us to remember that ghosts couldn't hurt us.

Okay. That was an eye-opener for me. My father, skeptic number one, telling us ghosts couldn't hurt us. It was somewhat calming to be able to talk about it, but I was terrified because we were in agreement that there really was something in the house. Something we couldn't see had changed Dad's mind.

* * *

Dad spent his next day off from work researching things at the County offices. He looked tired when he returned. Muttering something in a sarcastic tone about the "helpful" County offices, he laid papers out on the dining room table. He had maps and official documents from the Tax Assessor's Office. The first map he showed us was of our property. According to the property lines, the original property covered most of that corner of the valley. The map was dated 1877. The next map, dated 1897, showed property lines dividing this same parcel into numerous portions. The portion our house was on, was the size of our land plus the land of all of our immediate neighbors. The third and last map, dated 1973, showed the area as we knew it. Dad also consulted with our realtor Jack.

"I talked to Jack about who owned the property and about the history of the house," Dad explained. "He found that there was an old farm house where ours is now. The records showed it was built around 1903. In 1972, they tore down most of the old house. The floors were left in place, and the only full room that still stands is the dining room. The old floor is under the family room, kitchen, dining room, and the downstairs bathroom. Then they built the rest of our house around it. Parts of our house are from 1903!"

"Was there anything about who lived here?" questioned Mom.

"Not really. So, I checked the title records to try to find previous owners. The only strange thing was that in many of the deeds, it refers to one person when it describes the land. One person's name kept coming up. His name was Herbert Nelson."

"Maybe he died here. It could be him we are hearing," suggested Mom. "I think we should have a meeting with him. It couldn't hurt."

That evening at 8:30, we were to have our first discussion with "Herbert." We weren't sure it was Herbert in the house, but we thought it best to try to address the presence with this name. Together we walked from room to room talking to him, and introduced ourselves. Mom began "the talk" in the dining room.

"Hello Herbert? Herbert are you here? We want to talk to you. We know you live here, but we live here too. This is our house now. We won't try to get you out. You can stay here if you want, but we aren't leaving. We have to be able to get along in this house together. You treat us nice, and we'll treat you nice."

In each room, the speech was a little different. I hadn't expected it to help much, but the fact that we were all doing this together put me at ease. Afterward, we talked briefly and turned in early.

We did notice a marked decline in incidents after talking to Herbert. We began talking to him more often, as if he were a guest. We would hear a noise and say "Hi Herbert." By the end of August, most of our fear had subsided, and we thought our house problems were solved.

On September 23rd, Bruce was born. Lisa and I were excited to have a baby brother. Mom showed us how to change his diapers, and how to feed him his bottle. The small bedroom upstairs, next to Lisa's room, became his. The fall and winter months were full of watching this new cute creation trying to grasp a brand-new world. Bruce brightened the otherwise dreary winter days.

During these dark, cold days, we would often hear distant noises that sounded like somebody cleaning or looking for something. I heard someone moving around in the dining room one evening, but nobody was in there. We made it a point to keep all rooms closed to conserve on heating bills. Since most of the doors were closed, sounds came from these rooms frequently. As time passed, we tried to ignore it. It wasn't ignoring us.

DALE SCOTT

CHAPTER NINE

Unlike the previous two years, when spring arrived there was no strange car ominously waiting in the driveway. This time I saw something disturbing from the window in the small bedroom upstairs. It was a solitary figure standing in the middle of the hayfield, staring at the house. He was young, about six feet tall, pale, thin, and dressed in a black suit with a matching vest. The white shirt he wore was open at the "banded" collar. Had he been wearing a round black hat, I would have sworn he was Amish. Oddly, his collar-length dark brown hair was blown around by the wind, but the waist-high amber grass around him stood still in the warm air. He was staring at me with serious determination. I began shaking with fear. I opened the window and shouted, "What do you want?" He didn't move. I sprinted the 15 feet to the deck next to Mom and Dad's bedroom to shout again, but when I arrived, he was gone. I had a clear view of the field from the upstairs deck. There was no place to hide. From that angle, the grass could not conceal him. It took me three or four seconds to get to the deck, and in that amount of time, he couldn't have gotten far. The field was too big. I watched from the deck for a while longer, but saw no sign of him.

***

As spring slipped in under the drowsy eyes of a long winter, we began having fun with our new pet ghost. We would have "spook dinners" where friends were introduced to Herbert. Of course, it wasn't as if we were able to produce him and have him dance around or do tricks. Instead, if the conditions were right, the lights would flicker and we would call out "Herbert!" to get the lights back. Such things were not as dramatic for the guests around our dining room table. Sometimes people would challenge the notion that it was a ghost causing the lights to flicker. When they did so, the response came by way of the candles.

Our little candelabra held five candles, and they were lit most evenings when guests were dining. It closely resembled the brass and crystal chandelier centered over the table, but on a smaller scale. Often the candles would flicker and nearly go out entirely. It looked like someone was gently blowing on them. On such occasions, we made note that the windows were closed and there was no detectable draft.

The feeling in the dining room was different than in other rooms. When you entered, the sounds from the kitchen, family and living rooms seemed further away. It was an uneasy sensation when it became difficult to hear the sounds just beyond the threshold of the dining room door. It was a vulnerable feeling. The other rooms disappeared completely if the door was closed. The door itself was a light, hollow-core design that wasn't very soundproof. We didn't like to close the door to the dining room when we were inside.

The dinner parties continued, and the little appearances of Herbert's antics wowed the guests. They treated it as something fun to do. After a while, it became routine. The guests, hoping to see something new, would come for follow-up dinners, but would see the same things or nothing at all. Often, activity would take place when there were fewer guests. Doubts formed about the cause of the events. Most became skeptical that anything ghostly had occurred. Some guests wanted to challenge the existence of a ghost with devices to interact with the supernatural.

Much to Dad's disapproval, Mom agreed to let a friend come over for an experiment. Her name was Natalie, and she was one of Mom's customers. She dressed sloppily and I remember her as being in some sort of dreamy fog all the time. She had a sleepy look to her. Once she heard about our house, she begged Mom to invite her to dinner. It was after that dinner visit that she talked to Mom and proposed conducting the experiment.

Mom appeared to be in favor of having her over again and trying her ideas. But Dad didn't share Mom's curiosity. He didn't like Natalie. He said she was "bad luck" and "jinxed." Lisa and I were excited to have a séance in our own house, but that wasn't the intention. The plan was to try communicating with the spirit using a Ouija board. Although Dad was not happy about it, he finally acquiesced and Mom invited Natalie for dinner again.

The following week Natalie arrived with a cloth satchel and a bottle of wine. She set aside the satchel and we sat down to a nice meal. I could tell that Dad was irritated by anything that Natalie did or said, but he was trying his best to hide his irritation and be a good host. After dinner, and a moment to relax, Natalie brought her bag over and pulled out her Ouija board. She placed it in the middle of the table and the light of the dining room chandelier was replaced with candlelight. She lit a small cone of incense, and the smoke drifted upward filling my nose with an intoxicating aroma of sandalwood.

The air became still as we all sat around the dining room table. I don't think she really knew what she was doing, as it looked like it was her first time. Dad rolled his eyes and I detected a slight snort of a suppressed snicker. Evidently, Mom noticed it too. She kicked him under the table. We all placed one finger on the planchette while Natalie asked the questions.

"Who is here in the house with us?" she inquired.

Nothing.

"Will you speak to us?"

Nothing.

"Do you have something to tell us?"

The planchette trembled slightly, but we thought our hands were getting tired from holding them out and waiting.

"Who are you?"

Nothing.

"Are you Herbert?"

There was a slight tremble of the planchette and a flicker of the candles this time. We didn't think much of it. We waited. Nothing was happening. We were becoming impatient, and I think Dad was trying to keep from laughing at the ridiculous scene unfolding at our dining table. But Natalie had something else to try.

She took the Ouija board away and set it on the sideboard. From her bag, she produced a tattered deck of Tarot cards. She shuffled them while asking questions aloud.

"Who are you? Why are you here? What do you want? Will you talk to us?"

She dealt the cards into a cross pattern on the dining room table. Slowly she turned over each card. Among the cards that were dealt was the "Death" card. I don't know how anyone else felt, but I was instantly terrified.

"What does that mean?" I asked Natalie, trying to hide my fear.

"Oh, that doesn't mean 'death' literally. Its meaning is figurative only. For example, this card could signify that someone was on the threshold of a change. A new job, or shedding sadness and achieving happiness. Sometimes it could mean literal 'death,' but usually it does not. Let's just deal the cards again and forget about that one. Here, I'll do one on myself to show you."

While she was shuffling and dealing she began asking questions about her future.

"Will I become rich? What is in my future? Will I meet a tall, handsome man?"

The cards were turned over and she explained them to us.

"This one says that I'll have a long period of struggle with money, but this card says that I will eventually have more money than I have ever seen. This one says to be careful when it comes to romance. And the card next to it means romance is on a rocky road for me right now because I'm depicted romantically by the 'Fool' card. But this one says that in a couple of years the following card could happen. That card is 'The Lovers,' showing happiness romantically."

I didn't see how she made that kind of interpretation. From the look of things, I don't think Mom, Dad or Lisa did either. We held our comments, so as not to offend Natalie.

After the demonstration, she shuffled the cards and again directed the questions to the unknown spirit. Slowly she turned over the cards. The "Death" card appeared. Noticeably flustered, she scooped up the cards again and started shuffling.

"I know what the problem is," she said. "I am dealing the cards based on the spirit, and it is dead. I'll deal them for each of you individually to see what your future is here in the house."

She dealt for Dad first, asking questions about what would happen in the house for him. The cards were turned over. The "Death" card came up. She dealt again for Mom. The "Death" card came up. She dealt for me. The "Death" card came up.

"Okay. That's enough. We're stopping this right now,"

said Dad. "That deck is probably filled with 'Death' cards, right?"

"Only one," replied Natalie. "You don't believe me? Look for yourself!"

She fanned out the cards on the table. There was only one "Death" card in her deck.

After she left, we had a brief family meeting. I don't know if it was meant to calm us kids, or our parents. We agreed that whatever happened during Natalie's visit was probably coincidental, and that we would just forget about it. Again, we heard the "ghosts can't hurt you" speech. After Lisa and I went to bed, I could hear Mom and Dad talking for a long time until I fell asleep. Although they were trying to keep their voices down, I could hear that Dad was angry. Natalie never visited us again.

* * *

From that point forward, the presence in the house became increasingly aggressive. The attempted tarot card endeavor appeared to anger whatever it was. If it was trying to talk to us before, it definitely screamed for attention afterward. The first aggressive move happened to Mom's best friend one night.

Lynne worked with Mom. They went on many sales trips together, and they worked well as a team. Frequently, Mom would invite Lynne over for dinner. She commuted about fifty miles to work, and our house was 15 miles further, so after dinner one night, Mom suggested she stay at our house instead of driving home. Lynne accepted.

She did not believe in ghosts. Lynne actually laughed at us during dinner when we warned her the house was haunted. She went so far as to direct a smart remark into the air to show the resolve of her disbelief that a spirit was present to receive it. The rest of us looked at each other worried, wondering what ramifications this would bring. We hoped for the best, for Lynne's sake.

We made a place for Lynne that night. Lisa had a two-part trundle bed and she only used one part of it. Dad and I carried the other section of her bed downstairs to the family room area for Lynne to use. The bed was placed in front of the dining room door under a large painting of the Golden Gate Bridge.

Around three a.m. everyone awoke to Lynne screaming and pounding sounds from the family room. I ran out and found Lynne wrapped in her blankets shaking and pointing at the dining room door. My parents promptly sent me back to my room. I wanted to hear what happened, but Mom closed my bedroom door.

Moments later Mom opened the door again. I could hear Lynne. She was hysterical. It was decided that I would move upstairs and share Lisa's room, as Lynne would be staying in my bedroom. As I climbed the stairs, I could hear Lynne crying.

After Lynne left the next morning, I asked Mom and Dad about the incident. They said that something in the dining room rattled and pounded on the door as if struggling to get out. When Dad checked inside the dining room, no one was there.

Lynne never slept next to the dining room again, nor did she laugh at the notion of ghosts either. Although she continued to visit us for dinner on a regular basis, she behaved differently when in the dining room. She drank more gewürztraminer wine than before. Often she had too much.

Lynne also insisted on playing a cassette of soothing music with a train in the background during each visit. This may not seem out of the ordinary, but some of us became sick of listening to that tape after the first few dinners. Now to confess, I hid the tape. On Lynne's next visit, she looked for the tape. The panic on her face resembled the way she looked that night with the pounding on the dining room door. When we found another cassette tape to play with similar music, she calmed considerably. After her reaction, I felt ashamed to admit I had hidden the tape. I confided in Lisa, and we decided not to mention it.

Lisa and I became strong allies. When we moved into the house, the level of irritability between us increased. When items went missing, she and I argued regularly. Mom had a meeting with us to try to improve relations. She told us that we would always have each other to confide in for help, and we couldn't do that if we were constantly fighting. This talk changed us. As activities in the house became more frightening, we grew closer.

Our family life changed, with a noticeable edginess in all of us. Mom and Dad began smoking heavily. We were less talkative. The darkness of the night was contagious, and our moods reflected this. When guests visited, their presence was like a camp lantern. It was a distraction from the problems, with a feeling of safety when more people gathered.

Having a guest for dinner became a nightly ritual. This meant that the house needed to be spotless, and preparations began before guests would arrive with Mom or Dad from work. That was job was assigned to Lisa and me. The effort of entertaining a regular stream of "camp lanterns" was taking its toll on all of us. On one particular night, we had a call from Mom saying that she was on her way home with Lynne. Lisa and I looked at each other and our weary expressions said more than any words could. We cleaned the house quickly, started cutting up vegetables for a salad, and set the table. It was common for margaritas to be served. So, as I had assisted Mom when she made them in the past, I started a blender-full before anyone arrived, and had a glassful for myself. Dad was the first to arrive. He appeared drained from the day.

"Lynne's on her way with Mom," I said.

Dad dropped into the nearest chair without saying anything.

"Have a margarita. It seems to be helping," I offered.

Dad's eyes flashed at me in anger. It looked like he was going to punish me severely for drinking, but this look gave way to a sympathetic one as he accepted the drink.

"Is the house clean?" he asked.

"Yeah, and the bathroom is all set with new towels." Lisa confirmed.

"And I changed the sheets in my room in case she stays," I added.

At that moment, Mom and Lynne drove into the driveway in their separate cars. Our previous conversation was not mentioned, and the rest of the evening was uneventful. Not long after that night, Mom and Dad argued at length about the constant stream of dinner guests. We began having fewer guests, and more quiet family evenings. When our nights became calmer, the darkness crept back in and we could hear additional noises in the house.

DALE SCOTT

CHAPTER TEN

During these times sleep became a serious problem in our family. To some degree, we were afraid to close our eyes and drift off, or at least I was. I watched my black-and-white television until my body gave in to weariness around three or four o'clock in the morning. I couldn't bear to hear the sounds of the dark, like the frequent scratching on the outer wall below my window. It made no difference what programs were showing, it was something to watch, something to distract my fear. Back then, no channels were operating 24 hours a day. When one channel retired to the "off the air" tone, another would have to be found that was still broadcasting. On the latest running channels, often the programs were British soap operas. I didn't mind, and I actually grew to like the shows. As far as I was concerned, the best way to fall asleep was with the television on. To this day, I find it difficult to fall asleep without the television on.

Whenever I ventured out of my room to the kitchen for a late night snack, I would notice the television playing in Mom and Dad's room. The flicker from the set would fill the stairwell with an unearthly glow, while Johnny Carson cracked jokes with guests. In the morning, we would compare what we watched the previous night. Rarely were Lisa or I questioned about staying up so late. I believe Mom understood why we didn't get much sleep. She must have sensed our fear, or perhaps she had fears of her own.

Lisa was always pale because of her sleeplessness. She often complained of pounding on the walls at night in her room. She said they came in sets of three. I remember, although she does not, about an incident when she was screaming because someone was in the upstairs bathroom. Dad tried to calm her down, but she just kept repeating, "I saw it. I saw it. Check behind the door. I saw it." She would see faces in the windows at night. Dad would tell her it was impossible for someone to look into her upstairs window. She said she knew people couldn't get up to the windows, and that was why she was so afraid. Her safe haven was music. She would play the radio or her cassette player with a headset firmly over her ears, cover up with her blankets and stare at the wall next to her bed until she finally went to sleep.

One summer night, Lisa and I decided to stay up all night long. It was a challenge, but we thought it wouldn't be too difficult, since we regularly stayed up late. We stayed in her room watching TV, and playing board games. Around 3:00 a.m., the last television station signed off, and we switched to the radio. The snacks we made were long gone, and there was nothing else to do but read. As time passed, our fear grew. There was no obvious reason for the dread. The challenge to stay awake, turned into a deep terror to fall asleep. Lisa was sitting on her bed with her back against the wall and her eyes wide open, while I was sitting on the floor with my back against the opposite wall. Lisa turned off the radio. The room was silent. The air became visibly thick. A type of darkness was moving around the room. It wasn't like smoke; it was more like being underwater in the shallow end of a swimming pool, looking through the mass of water in the deep end.

"What is that?" asked Lisa, with a trembling voice.
"I don't know," I replied with difficulty.
"What should we do?"
"We could go to another room."
"I don't want to walk through it."
"I could get Dad," I offered.
"No! Don't leave me here."

So, we stayed where we were, watching the thickness move around. We kept talking to each other to reassure ourselves that it would be okay. The radio remained off. Sometime between 4:30 and 5:00 a.m. the thickness gradually faded. We stayed in our positions until first light, and then we left, almost running from the room.

One Saturday morning that summer, Lisa woke up late. The door to the upstairs bathroom was closed and the water was running. She figured that she missed her opportunity to use the bathroom before Mom started getting ready for work. After stopping in the downstairs bathroom, she went to the kitchen to make some breakfast. She was the only one in the kitchen. Dad left for work early, as was usual. I was outside in the garden. As Lisa poured some cereal into a bowl, she could hear Mom rushing around upstairs. She thought Mom must have been running late to be in such a hurry. Lisa glanced at the clock on the stove. It was 10:30. Mom was due at work by 10:00. While she was wondering about this, the phone rang. It was Mom. Lisa ran out of the house screaming, and although I tried to calm her, she would not go back inside until later that day. No one was found upstairs.

Gradually, everyone started seeing fleeting glimpses of things, and hearing pounding, pops or creaking. Pounding usually came from far rooms, while pops and creaking happened all around us. Often, I would catch some kind of movement out of the corner of my eye, while hearing some vague sound from that direction. Thinking it was Mom, Dad or Lisa, I would say something to them. When I would look up, no one was around.

***

That August was particularly hot. I remember because of the amount of time we spent in the pool. We set up a speaker in the dining room window to have the radio playing outside. We had friends over regularly, and actually slept on the deck by the pool a few nights. Bruce was carefully dipped in the pool for the first time. The garden was filled with black-eyed peas, corn, green beans, tomatoes, and squash. The summers were always a magical time, but more so that year. Outside of the noises in the house, we were really enjoying the end of summer.

Every Sunday after a full day of swimming and fun, we prepared a large dinner. We would barbeque, or Mom would cook fried chicken with mashed potatoes and gravy. Often we'd play music together in the living room. Mom on the piano, Dad and Lisa on guitars, I played the banjo and Bruce had his own way of "singing." We would gather in the far side of the living room. This was a newer part of the room which was added to the original old house. From here, the kitchen seemed far away, and although the same distance, the dining room appeared even further. We had fun on those nights. It was the kind of fun that lingered long after the music had stopped.

Toward the end of the month, we were jolted awake by loud pounding on the front door. I was the first to make it to the living room, followed by Dad coming from upstairs. As I approached the door, I felt instantly cold, and a pungent stench resembling rotting vegetables filled my nostrils. I thought I was going to be sick.

"Stay away from the door," Dad said in a whisper.

"Do you smell that?" I asked quietly.

"Smell what?"

"Come over here. Stand where I was. Do you feel the cold?"

"No."

"Can't you smell it?"

"No, I don't smell anything."

I tried to find the spot again, but it was gone. While I was trying to find it, the pounding started again. I jumped. Dad jumped. In my pursuit of the smell and cold, I had almost forgotten about the door.

"Who is it?" Dad shouted, but there was no response.

"Who the Hell is it, and what do you want?" he shouted.

There was a short silence, but then there was more pounding. It was getting louder.

"You call the sheriff. I'm getting my gun," Dad said in a serious, deliberate tone.

When Dad came back a few seconds later, he was loading his .38 revolver. He sent me upstairs and sat at the foot of the stairs watching the front door. The pounding continued with short intervals of silence. Soon the rotating pattern of the red lights from the sheriff's patrol car in the driveway filled the living room. The pounding continued, and then it suddenly stopped. Then there was a tapping at the door followed by "Sheriff's Department." Dad cautiously opened the door as I crept to the bottom stair to listen.

"Did you see him?" Dad asked.

"I didn't see anyone," the deputy explained.

"He was pounding on the door when you pulled up. I saw your lights in the driveway while he was pounding. Maybe you missed him and he's around the house."

"Sir, take a look at my car."

I looked through the window while they were talking. The deputy had driven around our circular driveway in the opposite direction than most people did so that when he parked, the car was facing the front door. In addition to the flashing lights and the headlights, he had a spotlight on the roof of the car illuminating the entire front yard.

"If someone was at your door when I pulled up, it would be impossible to not be seen. I'll look around the house for you, but I don't think there is anyone here."

He checked all around the outside of the house, but found nothing. After a calming down period, we all tried to go back to sleep. Lisa agreed to let me stay in her room. I kept thinking about the pounding, the cold feeling and the stench.

* * *

In September we went "camping." We didn't actually use tents and cook our meals over a fire, instead we stayed in a rustic cabin next to a lake several hours north. It was a secluded place with other cabins, but the season had ended, and we were practically the only people at the resort. The owner was welcoming. He was a large man that drove a dark green Lincoln Continental. With his advice, we found many good fishing spots. The days were relaxing, and best of all, we didn't have to put up with the strange noises of our house. For one week, we were able to catch our breath. We dreamed of having that kind of peace at home.

CHAPTER ELEVEN

That winter was the first Christmas Bruce actually attempted to open presents. I don't think he knew what it was about, beyond the flashing lights of the tree and the colors of the packages, but he looked excited, if not bewildered. Dad received a lot of protest from Lisa when he took a photo of her first thing Christmas morning while she listened to a tape she had received. She was wearing a large headset, and an oversized white cotton robe. Her hair was sticking out in many directions, her face barely visible. You could definitely tell she was hardly awake. She was not happy about that picture.

In January, I caught a nasty flu that kept me home from school for two weeks. It was exceptionally cold for California that winter, and everything looked bleak. There was little light, with lots of cold rain. The absence of daylight cast a deeper gloom everywhere in the house. I couldn't stand to watch the boring things on the five, and sometimes six, stations that our television received semi-clearly. The radio played depressing songs about disenchantment of love and failures of love affairs. And to top it off, the flu magnified the feeling of gloom and despair. I needed something to cheer me up. I needed to get well.

One evening, as I was recovering and feeling much better, Mom and Dad took us to Michelle's Restaurant. Contrary to the French name, it was a fancy Italian restaurant that offered family-style dining. The warm, cozy feeling inside was a contrast to the pouring rain outside. While we had minestrone soup, Mom commented on how nice it was not to have to put up with Herbert at dinner. We left the restaurant feeling very satisfied, with doggie bags to bring home for snacking later.

The car ride north was near silent. We dreaded going back to a dark house. The rain and the darkness enhanced the secluded feeling. Once again, we were alone, our fears increasing.

When we arrived, the phone was ringing. It was Gramma. Mom answered the phone and addressed her in the formal way of "Mother" as she usually did. Dad was asked to join the conversation on the second phone. After their conversation, Mom and Dad told us that Gramma and Grampa were moving back to California from Missouri.

That winter had been particularly bitter, and they missed the warmer California climate. They would be staying with us until their house sold in Missouri, and then they could afford to purchase a new one in California. In a couple of weeks, Dad was to fly to Missouri and drive their car back here, pulling a U-Haul trailer with their furniture inside. Gramma and Grampa would take a airplane flight. We were all very enthusiastic about their return. There was great optimism in having more people on our side to help us face our fears.

Dad arranged to be away from work, and handled all of the plans for plane tickets and the rental of the U-Haul trailer. The whole move took one week to accomplish. It was truly like a holiday when they returned.

When they arrived, we greeted them with a large welcome home dinner. A big hole in our lives had opened up when they left for Missouri a few years earlier, and now was filled with warmth and love again. My grandparents had many stories to tell about the difference in the weather and updated us on how our relatives were doing. We shared stories as well.

We explained about the noises around the house. They thought it was funny. Gramma didn't seem affected by our accounts, and Grampa had a few of his own. He told us of a job he took while they were in Missouri, as a night watchman in a casket factory. He said that he would find lights on in the casket building shop in the middle of the night, which he had turned off on his last round. It was a problem because the switch for the lights was on the other side of the large shop, and he would have to find his way back through the room in the dark, while avoiding wood and tools that were left after the workday ended. He also described how on one night, an unfinished casket was open. This wasn't unusual, except that he wasn't sure if it was open when he walked through on the previous hour's round. "I may have been wrong about that, but I didn't stick around to find out," he recounted. Gramma laughed and said he was silly.

Spring brought an easiness that we had not felt the previous years. I shared Lisa's room, and Gramma and Grampa stayed in the downstairs bedroom. As the flowers bloomed, I dreaded the arrival of the spring visitor in the driveway or in the field. For some reason, the visitor never arrived. There was, however, the sound of footsteps in the gravel driveway with nobody present to create them. Since there was no noticeable spring visitor, I thought something had shifted and we may have a decrease in activity from Herbert. I was wrong.

Grampa created a large vegetable garden when the weather got warmer. He added okra and pumpkins to the vegetables we grew in the past, and liked to water the garden by hand in the early evening. He would have his strong iced tea, and Gramma would sit in a patio chair to keep him company while he watered the newly planted rows.

On one occasion, I was developing a roll of Kodak Tri-X 400 ASA black-and-white film for the school newspaper. Photography was a hobby I learned quickly, and I took my new position on the school paper seriously. After feeding the film onto a reel and placing it into the developing tank in complete darkness, I filled the stainless steel film tank with chemicals at the kitchen sink. While I waited for the chemicals to process the film, I could see Gramma and Grampa out by the garden. I felt much safer with them at home with us.

The pounding on the wall started again. It sounded like it was upstairs in Lisa's room. I was the only one inside the house. Lisa and Bruce were with Mom shopping, and Dad was at work. I dumped the fixer solution from the tank and put water in it quickly. Gramma and Grampa had not experienced any noises as yet, and hopefully I could get them in the house fast enough to hear the pounding first hand.

"Gramma, the pounding on the wall, it's happening right now. Come on, you have to hear it," I called while approaching the garden.

Grampa set the water nozzle down and we all went into the house. The pounding had stopped. We waited, but nothing happened. After about five or ten minutes, Grampa went back outside to resume watering, and Gramma waited for a little while longer. There was no further noise. Mom came home and our mini-vigil ended. Gramma thought it was funny.

* * *

We acquired a goat. His name was William. I would have picked a name other than the cliché for goats, but someone had already given him that name. It was too late. He had a coarse gray coat, a long beard, and two eight-inch horns. Although he would eat almost anything, William preferred cigarettes and beer (a bad habit learned from the previous owners). The reason we bought him was so he'd eat the tall grass in the field to keep the fire danger down. We soon found that he was obsessed with the house. William learned how to get past the gate from the field and would charge toward the house from different angles. Then, he'd butt the house with his horns and bleat loudly. So to prevent him from moving so quickly, we put a weight on a chain attached to his collar. He could move freely and not hurt himself. His behavior was so erratic; we tried to steer clear. Lisa gave him the nickname of "Devil Goat." I would tack on "Goat from Hell." Soon, we just called him by that collective nickname: "Devil Goat-Goat from Hell."

During this time, Grampa had a call from Missouri announcing there was an offer on their house. While things were being ironed out, and escrow started, they began looking for a new home nearby. My parents tagged along. On the nights when they were gone, the noises would occur on a regular basis. It didn't take long for us to notice the noises stopped when Gramma and Grampa were in the house. Lisa and I discussed it, and concluded that either Herbert was afraid of our grandparents, or he just didn't want to risk scaring them because of their old age. The hope that Herbert was a kind entity and was staying silent for the latter reason gave us some sense of calm. The noises continued when we were alone in the house, however. We were getting used to them again. Then, it learned my name.

The first time this happened it startled me. I was washing dishes in the middle of the day with the water running. From behind me, I heard my dad call my name. Startled, I jumped and turned around. Dad often liked to play similar jokes on us, but this time he wasn't present. I looked out the window, and he was with Grampa in the garden. I was alone. I must have imagined it, or the running water produced an auditory illusion; therefore I put it aside.

The next time it happened, I was vacuuming the family room area. Once again, the voice came from behind me in a moderate volume. I stopped the vacuum cleaner and looked around. This time I figured it must be something with that area of the house and possible echoes. I continued vacuuming when I heard the voice again, this time slightly louder. Still, nobody was there. I started the machine, and heard the voice a fourth time, with a firm tone. There was no mistaking it. I switched off the vacuum cleaner and called out.

"What? What do you want?" I yelled out.

Dad came running down the stairs from his bedroom. "What's the matter?"

"Someone keeps calling me. Someone was calling my name when I was vacuuming."

"Maybe your ears are just playing tricks on you," he said, and went back upstairs.

Ignoring the voice was difficult. No matter what the cause, it scared the hell out of me.

Outside, I would hear the voice while mowing the lawn. I heard it most often when I would use the power weeder around the rose garden. Therefore, I would hurry when working around there. I felt uneasy when the line would break or wear out, causing me to stop and pull more line from the cutting head, slowing my progress. It only said my name. I have never heard the voice since leaving that house. Later I found that it called Lisa's name to her too, but she never mentioned it at the time.

In mid-July, Gramma and Grampa moved into a nice mobile home in a retirement community nearby. We helped move the stored furniture and boxes from the back of our long garage, into a corner space lot in Meadowcreek Mobile Home Park. The park was in a large field between the highway and the railroad tracks. It was a nice place to live. Outside of the chirping birds, and an occasional "hello" from a neighbor, it was a quiet area. In our house, however, things began getting louder.

This was the summer the 'door slamming' started. Dad said it was the wind, but many times the doors were to rooms with closed windows. It would never be a door right next to you. It was always a door in another part of the house. The first few times it happened to me, I would go and find the doors closed. After a while, it seemed a waste of time. Others in the house heard it. I accepted Dad's explanation of wind causing the doors to slam because I didn't want to think of the alternative. If it wasn't the wind, then Herbert appeared to be getting more aggressive. So, I ignored it. We ignored it.

Around the end of August, the slamming door problem took on a new twist. I was home alone when I heard a door upstairs slam closed. I ignored it. An hour or so later, I was taking some newly washed towels upstairs to put in the linen cupboard. I went up to the upstairs hallway, opened the cupboard and put away the towels. When I finished, I started downstairs. At the top of the stairs, it struck me that none of the upstairs doors were closed. I turned and confirmed this to be true. I checked the doors and all were wide open. I checked the windows. All were closed. "I don't want to know this," I repeated over and over as I went downstairs to the kitchen. Upstairs, a door slammed; this time louder.

In my young adult mind, I tried to grapple with the logic of what was happening. Why us, and damn it, why me? Why was it calling my name? It wanted something, and as each year passed without any resolution to Herbert's demands, he seemed to get more impatient and angry. What did he want from us? Was he trying to tell us something? I wanted to understand the presence, but was afraid of what I would find.

CHAPTER TWELVE

Activity in the house increased over the winter, and so did our vocal opposition to it. No longer were we cheerfully talking to Herbert (or whoever it was). Now we yelled back. Oddly, there was no complaint among us about our new vocal behavior. We understood each other. We'd had enough. Now we were directing our irritability toward the presence. On one occasion, when I was alone downstairs, I ended up shouting foul obscenities at the distant sounds. While this was a great way to vent frustration, it did little to stop the activity.

That winter it flooded. The nearby river flowed over its banks and flooded many towns. Our area was under water because of the river and an antiquated storm drain system situated around nearby farms. When the water reached two feet above the lawn and met the top step of the front porch, I took our old rowboat and tied it up next to the front door. Luckily, that was the high mark, and the water receded during the night without entering our house. That season, the plants outside began growing sooner and flowers began blooming early because of the added rainfall and ground moisture. It was like an early spring.

The annual spring visitor this time was not seen but

heard. It sounded like a large car or truck pulling into the driveway. Without visual evidence, the prospect of convincing the Sheriff something was there did not look good. I didn't want to get in trouble for a false alarm. So I checked through the windows again, but saw no car. I went outside and looked down the long driveway, but still no vehicle.

If this was indeed the spring visitor, it became a recurring one. The invisible car continued to arrive in the driveway sporadically, at different times of the day. As the weeks progressed, it began arriving in the evenings. Eventually, it only came at night. At night you could see headlights.

The first time the invisible car arrived in the late hours, Lisa, Bruce and I were home alone. We were watching TV in the family room when we heard a car and saw the lights. Mom was due home, so we assumed it was her. After a couple of minutes, she had not come in. I thought that she might have groceries to bring in. I went to the back door to help her, but there were no cars in the driveway. Lisa and I both saw the car arrive. Just as we were beginning to panic, Mom arrived. It was a relief, but it didn't always happen that way.

Usually the outside lights around the back door and driveway were off. When an unexpected car would arrive, we'd turn off the lights inside the house and peek out to see who it was. If we couldn't see a car, we would carefully open the wooden sliding pocket door to the back porch enabling us to see through the windows to the driveway and back step area.

The silence and darkness were terrifying. Long periods of time would pass while we waited for a sound or a bit of light. None would come. The "car" would not leave, and after a while, we would give in and quickly turn on all of the outside lights. No one was ever there. We worried someone unseen would be lurking in the darkness just beyond the reach of the porch lights.

I still have nightmares about waiting and listening to this day. I can see the dark windows of the back porch; afraid that a face would appear, like an answer on a Magic Eight Ball toy. In certain versions of the nightmare, I go outside to get something from Mom's car, or the barn, and I find a person hiding, or the mystery car.

* * *

Money was a problem. Since things weren't getting any better with Herbert, Mom and Dad decided it would be best to sell the house. They even entertained the idea of moving to Missouri, like Gramma and Grampa did. For a while, we subscribed to the local paper of a small Missouri town. The house was put on the market in early April. We kept the house immaculate, as well as the pool, in case prospective buyers wanted a tour of the property. Pictures were taken for the ads in the local paper. Many people came, but there were no reasonable offers. After a few months, it was clear that we weren't meant to sell the house. It seemed as if there was unfinished business between the house and us.

CHAPTER THIRTEEN

One morning Dad questioned all of us. He appeared as if he had been awake since very early morning hours, if not longer. That would explain his irritation.

"Were you up late last night?"

"No," I replied.

"So it wasn't you playing the piano at two o'clock this morning?"

"No, I was asleep."

"Did you turn on the spotlight over the piano after we all went to bed?"

"No, I went to sleep before you guys."

"What's the matter?" Mom asked.

While we sat around the little table in the kitchen, Dad told us what happened.

"I woke up in the middle of the night. It was around two in the morning. I heard someone playing the piano. I got up and went downstairs to see who it was. The music stopped when I reached the stairs. I walked downstairs to the living room. Nobody was there."

"It was probably just a dream," Mom said.

"That's what I thought. But the music was still playing after I got out of bed. Plus, when I got downstairs, the spotlights above the piano were on full. I turned them off myself before going to bed. There was nobody downstairs—I looked. Everyone else seemed to be asleep."

Finding a light on was not new to us, but music playing in the middle of the night was. Since our whole family is musical, it was not strange to hear the piano playing in the next room. After Dad's experience, I began to question any music playing. Most of the time when I asked Mom about music being played late at night, she would confirm that she had been playing piano. Occasionally, she had not. None of us had.

This posed a tremendous problem to me. If I wanted to get water or a snack from the kitchen at night, would I be serenaded as I walked through the living room? That really frightened me. Still, I couldn't let my fear prevent me from doing something as simple as going to the kitchen. Therefore, I would plan my path, hold my breath, and rush to the light switch, praying for the florescent bulbs to flicker with life. "Don't look over there," I would repeat to myself, under my breath. There are no late night movies that could deliver the kind of suspense like the possibility of our piano playing on its own in the dark living room.

It was on one of these kitchen sorties that I first heard another recurring event. Although what I feared most was the piano, I had no idea that there could be something darker. Looking back, it did help to explain some of the activities, and possibly, why Herbert was still there.

It was 2:45 in the morning. I was watching a late movie from the early 1970's about somebody bringing a witness back for trial. The mission at hand, for me, was to obtain something to eat from the kitchen. Somewhere between "don't look at the piano," and "light switch-light switch," I heard someone in the hallway above. It wasn't someone walking, but rather a heavy staggering sound followed by something scraping the wall. A thunderous crash followed that shook the entire house. Trying to remember the first aid training from school, I ran upstairs. There was nobody in the hallway. Bruce was asleep. Lisa was asleep. Mom and Dad were asleep. Shaking, partly from fear and partly from confusion, I went back downstairs to the kitchen to get the snack and return to the movie. I thought the only way to handle it was to go back to business as usual and pretend it didn't happen, although my heart was still pounding.

I missed a bit of the movie, and was trying to calm down from the excitement. I finished my snack, and when the movie went to a commercial break, mustered up all the courage I could and returned the plate to the kitchen. It was 3:15 am. As I passed under the hallway on the way back to my room, I heard the staggering again.

My skin grew cold. I began to shiver. My eyes watered uncontrollably. I could not breathe. While the room grew smaller around me, I made a conscious effort to take in air. Warmth returned to my skin, and the room returned to its actual size. I continued to shake while I wiped my eyes.

The staggering was followed by the scraping, and then the crash that made all of the downstairs windows rattle. I ran back upstairs. Deep within me, I knew that I wouldn't find anything upstairs. I didn't. Everyone was sleeping. Everyone was okay, except me.

The next morning I was the one with all the questions. I asked if anyone fell out of bed during the night. Nobody remembered having done so. I felt alone. No one had heard the sounds but me. I had experienced a horror I could not explain. Up to this point, the occurrences had been manageable, but the magnitude of the crashing sound, how it shook all the windows, and happening in the stillness of the middle of the night with no one else hearing it--this was terrifying.

The staggering sounds continued that summer. It was always at 2:45 and 3:15 in the morning during very warm weather. Sometimes the sounds were accompanied with large cold pockets of air that stank of mildew and rot in the family room. It sounded like someone having a heart attack and falling; or perhaps someone being struck or killed, then staggering to their final fall. Eventually, everyone heard what I had experienced, and I was no longer alone in my fear.

Lisa also experienced things on her own. She always watched channel two and only that channel on the television. One day I asked her why she didn't watch the other channels.

"I try to," she explained, "but the channel always gets changed back by itself."

"There must be something wrong with how you're switching the channel." I turned the dial until the set clicked on channel four. "See, it's working just fine."

"No, it will change back," she said, as I turned to leave. The program on the TV went to a commercial break. As I was exiting the room, I heard the station call letters: "KTVU, channel two, San Francisco."

I wheeled around. Lisa was still in her seat, looking at me. The TV was about ten feet away, and the indicator on the dial read "2."

"Told you," she said. It must have been difficult to be the youngest (besides our baby brother Bruce) when the older people didn't believe you.

One warm summer day, Mom, Bruce and I were in town, while Dad and Lisa stayed home. Dad wanted to work in the garden on his day off, and Lisa was supposed to clean her room. While upstairs, she heard Dad talking to a man in the kitchen, whose voice she didn't recognize. After quite some time they stopped talking. Lisa walked to the kitchen for something to drink. No one was downstairs. She could see Dad out in the garden weeding in the far corner. She went to him and asked about the conversation. He replied that he had not been in the house for several hours and no one had visited.

Another evening, Lisa went to check on Bruce while he was sleeping in his room. We all heard a thud and then Lisa screaming. We rushed upstairs. Lisa was on the floor in the hallway next to the bathroom door, rubbing her head. Her scream woke Bruce and he began to cry. While Dad helped Lisa, Mom checked on Bruce.

"What happened?" Dad asked.

"I ran into the bathroom door," said Lisa.

"Are you okay?"

"Yeah, I just hit my head pretty hard."

"What was the screaming about then?"

"It was nothing."

"It wasn't 'nothing.' You woke up Bruce, and we all came rushing up here. We thought something terrible happened to you."

"I was just afraid."

"Afraid of what?" Mom asked.

"Afraid of whoever closed the bathroom door."

"What do you mean?" asked Mom.

"When I came up to check on Bruce, I was going to use the bathroom too. The bathroom door was open when I turned on the light in Bruce's room. I checked on him, and he was asleep. I turned off his light and walked out of his room toward the bathroom. Since it was dark, I couldn't see that the door had closed, and I walked right into it."

"You must have made a mistake about the door being open," said Dad.

"No! I didn't," Lisa said firmly.

"Alright, that's enough," said Dad, closing the issue.

* * *

Sometime that summer, Mom and Dad took the house off the market, regardless of our financial difficulties. So, as an illogical plan to help with the family finances, I considered the possibility of finding buried treasure somewhere on the property. The logical jump for me was to think it was possible, with a house this old, for someone to have hidden something. If it were of enough value, I could save the day and make it easier on all of us. But where would someone hide a treasure? There would have to be a permanent marker, like a tree, and in a protected place. After a couple of days of consideration, I decided on the rose garden.

In one corner there were three boulders surrounding a small piece of dirt with a tall young redwood tree on one side. The boulders were approximately four feet long, two feet wide and two feet tall. Two were lying on their sides, and the third was standing upright like a sentinel. It would be difficult to move these stones, but there was just enough space between them to hide something. I thought it was a good place to start looking.

The next day I started digging. I scraped off the weeds and grass between the boulders. As I began creating a hole, Dad came out of the house with his coffee cup to find out what I was doing.

"I'm looking for buried treasure," I said.

"Buried treasure...hmm. Aren't you a little old for that? Why here?" he asked.

"Something just told me this was a good place; between the rocks. Besides, if you were going to bury something valuable, can you think of any better place around the house?"

"No. I guess you're right. Don't dig anywhere near the roses though, or your mother will kill you."

The excavation continued, with the blessing of my father, and after a lot of digging and probing, I hit something solid. "A box!" I thought--but no. It was only a piece of concrete. I decided to find the edge of the concrete, and get it out of there to continue my digging. An hour passed as I cleared dirt from the top of the concrete. Eventually I found the edges of the slab, but I would not be removing it. The slab measured almost six feet long by two foot wide and was oval in shape. I was on the verge of giving up the search, but decided to take a break and have some lunch. Afterward, I returned with renewed curiosity.

The edges of the slab were not even. This concrete had not been poured into a form, as is done when making sidewalks or patios. It had rough edges. It looked like someone had filled a hole with the concrete then covered it up with dirt. If I couldn't move the concrete, I'd dig under to see if there was something hidden underneath. I began making a mini-tunnel under the slab with a hand spade, and clearing the loose dirt with my hands. After some time, I felt something strange while clearing dirt. I pulled it up and shook the dirt off to reveal a brown-colored bone.

"A chicken bone? No. A dog? No. Cat? No. What could it be?" I thought as I was looking it in my hand. "HAND!" I exclaimed aloud, dropping the bone. I placed it on the back of my left hand. It was the same size and dimension as the bones in the back of my hand. One bone was not enough evidence. I needed more. From the same hole, alongside the slab, I pulled out three similar bones including smaller bones, possibly finger segments. Still, I needed more. A skull would be plenty of evidence.

I started excavating at the end of the slab pointing towards the roses. Immediately, I found a molar tooth. "Okay. That's enough. Time to talk to Dad," I told myself. I collected the bones in a plastic sandwich bag and went inside to show Dad what I found.

"It's probably just an animal," was Dad's first comment.

"But look at how these bones match the back of my hand," I said, as I demonstrated.

"Probably just coincidence."

"Okay, how about this?" I produced the molar tooth.

"You found that too?"

"Yes, and it was under the top edge of the slab where a head would be if a body was buried there. The hand bones were under the side of the slab where a hand would be."

"Did you find a skull?"

"No. I stopped digging. I thought we should probably

call the sheriff before I dig further."

"We don't need that kind of trouble. Take those bones and bury them where you found them," Dad said firmly.

I went back to the slab, and dropped the baggie down the hole alongside the concrete slab where I found the hand bones. After it was covered we didn't talk about the slab. It wasn't until we moved away that we discussed the body in the rose bed at any length. Mom still has difficulty believing it happened. Was that the final resting-place for Herbert? Was he buried in the rose bed because he was the victim of foul play? Who else knew he was there? Was he the one staggering and falling in the upstairs hallway in the middle of the night? Was this the unfinished business we had with the house?

CHAPTER FOURTEEN

As summer was ending, Mom and Dad received a surprise offer for the house. It had been off the market for some time. The interested buyer was a developer who needed our property in addition to the adjacent parcel already purchased. The success of the development depended on owning our land. He offered to pay far more than our original asking price. Mom and Dad accepted. Under the provisions of the purchase agreement, we were able to stay in the house a few months, while looking for a new home. We found a nice house on the outskirts of town, and once escrow closed, we would move. We started packing early while we waited.

During this time, the goat got loose from his "ball and chain." The first thing he did was to charge the house. He kept butting it with his head. It looked like he believed he could knock the building over. Perhaps it was foreshadowing the fate of the house in the hands of the developer. At any rate, it reminded us that we were not able to take William to the new house. We reattached his chain and he went back to eating grass.

That night we had a strong windstorm. The house shook, the windows rattled, and the trees swayed. The howling wind was haunting. Sometime in the middle of the night while we were asleep, the large poplar tree by the pond gave in to the power of the wind and fell. The next morning Dad found William, under the tree trunk. Before the rest of us woke, he buried the goat in the field. Dad told us that the tree landed on his head, believing William hadn't suffered.

After the tree was cut up and removed, I found the goat's two horns. The tree did indeed land on his head. We started thinking that something guided that tree to kill the goat. It appeared to have aimed for William and not just a chance occurrence.

On one of the nights after the tree fell, Mom woke up to see a vaporous shape floating in the far corner of the bedroom. She said it hovered for a while, then drifted slowly toward the hallway. She lay paralyzed for a moment, staring at the vapor as it stayed next to the bedroom door. Before she could wake Dad, it faded away.

Finally, moving day came. It happened quickly. We had endured many unearthly events, but now it was time to cross out of this world and into one without flickering lights, doors slamming on their own and mysterious visitors. We all thought about this during our transition out of the house and into normalcy.

We cleared out every building. The house was clean. The yards were in good shape. I asked Dad why we were going to all this extra effort if everything would be torn down to build new houses. His reply was that this was the proper way to leave things. Afterward, the house looked ready for new owners to move in and enjoy.

We left on a Friday. After the last box was loaded onto the borrowed delivery truck, we stood together to survey the house and land we had lived on for several years. We reflected on the good times, and the difficulties. It had been a test that helped us to grow as a family. In a way, we were leaving a big piece of ourselves behind. Soon it would be nothing but dirt. There would be no looking back.

EPILOGUE

We drove by the house a few months later to find that the developers had done nothing to the property. Thinking that the buildings would be demolished and the land graded, we were surprised to see that everything was still standing. We drove down the driveway, and turned the car to face the house. It looked just as it had when we first discovered it. The yards were overgrown. The house looked empty, forsaken, and sad. It was as if we hadn't been there at all. This is the last image I have of the house. It was demolished the following month.

Somehow, I knew when it was torn down. I had a dream, one night, that the house had no windows or doors anymore. The following day a friend called to say that our house was gone. With a sigh of relief and sadness, a small tear welled up in my eye. It was over.

* * *

I still live in the area. While writing this, I wanted to research the property and the various owners since the late 1800's. I asked my dad about the documents he found listing the previous owners, but he had discarded the paperwork years after we left. My mother didn't have any paperwork, but owned many photos of the house. So, I went on a quest to verify who once owned the property, with hopes of finding a "Herbert".

I found a wealth of information at local libraries and the County offices. Everyone I met was helpful, and I was surprised to find how much fun it was to do this kind of research.

I discovered the maps which Dad found. The earliest one was from 1877. A large section of land (which included our land) had been owned by a prominent settler. On that property, he built one of the earliest houses in the area. I found a photograph of the house taken many years later. That particular house could be seen across the field from our back yard. (It is not there now.)

The large property shown on the 1877 map has been parceled into many lots and is now a densely populated community. This includes a Wal-Mart/Home Depot/Office Depot shopping center in one corner, with a school and fire department in another.

The next map was drawn in 1897. In this map, our land was part of a larger parcel that covered the lands of all the neighboring fields. Lastly, there were maps from the years my family lived there, showing the property lines as we remembered.

After reviewing the maps, I traced back through the title deeds. All of the deeds referred to the land as "being owned by Herbert Nelson" when defining boundaries. Even my parents' deed included archaic measuring specifications (now they are just referred to by parcel numbers). Rods, chains, meridians were all used to describe the property lines. Herbert and his wife bought the property in 1910, and from that point forward, all deeds used that purchase as a reference.

I then found Herbert's deed. I also discovered deeds dating back to 1898 (around the time that the larger lot was split into the parcels we knew). I continued searching forward in time in the Recorder's logbooks, and came across a listing I had only suspected I would find. It was a deed transfer from the estate of Herbert to his wife. When I read the actual transaction document on microfilm, it answered my questions. Herbert had died while living in the house. All possessions were listed that were being transferred, including farm implements and a wagon. There were notations about costs associated with an illness, funeral expenses and actual date of death.

Only one cemetery existed in the area of that time, and I suspected Herbert was buried there. I drove to the cemetery office and inquired about him, and they pointed me towards his grave. A simple wooden replacement marker had his name on it. No further information was available.

Next, I drove to the County offices in search of a death certificate. I wanted to know if the staggering sounds in the upstairs hallway had anything to do with his death. Herbert's certificate was found on microfilm. The clerk printed it for me. The cause of death was listed as a heart attack. Under "occupation", it stated "printer". He was not an old man.

Further digging found a local newspaper article, dated the day after his death. Herbert was a typesetter, and his office was about 30 miles from his home. He was working at night, and was discovered the next morning. The article went on to say that the doctor who responded said Herbert had been dead for several hours. This could place the time of death around 2:00-3:00 am.

Here is my theory. The cause of death was consistent with the staggering and falling sounds heard upstairs in the late evening hours, as was the time of death. Perhaps the sounds were a message. Perhaps it was Herbert's heart attack replaying each time we heard the staggering.

The newspaper article also alluded that he moved to our rural area from the city to slow down or prepare for retirement. He must have loved the place as we did. To have his dreams interrupted in this way, I would imagine that he didn't want to leave. It was his house. It was his destiny.

The other unresolved question concerned the bones found in the rose garden. In seeing how the land was divided, and the time period of these divisions, I had a theory. In the late 1800's, many farms had family cemeteries in secluded areas on their land. In the 1870's, when the house across the field from ours was built (the original house on the large parcel), our rose garden would have been far enough away to serve that purpose. There were older trees in the area, thus telling me it had not been cultivated for hay. It was a perfect spot for such a family cemetery. My theory is that the bones were discovered during later construction (perhaps around 1903 when our original house was built). When they found them, they re-buried them, and poured concrete to protect them. To further prevent disturbance, large boulders were placed around the spot.

It is both unnerving and a relief to find our suspicion of Herbert's unexpected death was accurate, and that we possibly shared the house with him. The archived records seemed to point in that direction. Looking at the official documents and newspapers made me wonder what kind of life his family led.

The day I found his grave, I stood before the simple white wooden marker with only his initials and a number painted in black upon it. Here was the man who was a part of our family's lives for many years, yet we never actually met him as he was no longer living. Whether it was his spirit in our house could never be proven. Still, I felt compelled to say a few quiet words to him. I told him that I was sorry to hear the he died alone. Sorry that he did not get to live in his new house for very long, and that he was taken from his wife and family. I told him that if it was him in the house with us all of those years, that it was quite an experience sharing that house with him. Either way, we enjoyed living in the house that he once lived in, and we would always remember our days there. I wished him peace.

Once a person experiences these types of occurrences, it is impossible to deny the existence of unseen forces, whatever the cause. Having lived in this house and have so much happen, each of the members of my family now have a new awareness of things termed "paranormal." We learned to trust the physical sensations, such as pressure in the temples, heaviness weighing on the face, a coldness in the chest or unexpected sudden nausea, as cues to pay attention. For example, once on a tour of a famous mansion in Rhode Island, my father mentioned feeling some of those sensations. He looked up, and a person walked past him and into a long wood-paneled hallway. When he looked down the hallway, the person was gone. Or, the time I visited a client's house for dinner, and felt strong sensations next to the kitchen. As the feelings were too powerful to ignore, I asked what had happened. She explained that a previous owner was found dead in the place where I was standing. When visiting a house for the first time, my mother or sister will often turn to me and ask if I could feel those familiar sensations like we did in our house.

Living in our old house in the country has left a lasting impression on everyone in my family, and although people may not believe us, we know what happened there. To us it is undeniable. Would I live in a house like that again if I had a choice? The answer is simple: no.

* * *

Things are different on our little patch of hayfields now. On our old property, there is a modern housing development where each of the nine houses carries a price tag twice the amount the developer paid us for the land. The only remaining feature is an oak tree on the edge of the property that was not far from our pool. I have driven past there a handful of times for brief nostalgic visits. A house stands exactly where our house once stood. It is often for sale.

ABOUT THE AUTHOR

Dale Scott lives with his wife in picturesque rural Northern California.

Made in the USA
Las Vegas, NV
27 April 2025